The Cambridge Introduction to
Charles Dickens

JON MEE

CAMBRIDGE
UNIVERSITY PRESS

CAMBRIDGE UNIVERSITY PRESS
Cambridge, New York, Melbourne, Madrid, Cape Town, Singapore,
São Paulo, Delhi, Dubai, Tokyo, Mexico City

Cambridge University Press
The Edinburgh Building, Cambridge CB2 8RU, UK

Published in the United States of America by Cambridge University Press, New York

www.cambridge.org
Information on this title: www.cambridge.org/9780521676342

© Jon Mee 2010

First published 2010

Printed in the United Kingdom at the University Press, Cambridge

A catalogue record for this publication is available from the British Library

Library of Congress Cataloguing in Publication data
Mee, Jon.
    The Cambridge introduction to Charles Dickens / Jon Mee.
       p.   cm. – (Cambridge introductions to literature)
    Includes bibliographical references and index.
    ISBN 978-0-521-85914-1 (hardback) – ISBN 978-0-521-67634-2 (pbk.)
    1. Dickens, Charles, 1812–1870–Criticism and interpretation.   2. Dickens, Charles,
    1812–1870–Literary style.   3. Dickens, Charles, 1812–1870–Knowledge–London
    (England)   4. Dickens, Charles, 1812–1870–Political and social views.
    5. Dickens, Charles, 1812–1870–Adaptations.   I. Title.   II. Series.
    PR4588.M44 2010
    823'.8–dc22
    2010021908

ISBN 978-0-521-85914-1 Hardback
ISBN 978-0-521-67634-2 Paperback

For my sister, Rebecca Richmond, and Sharmila, dearest of readers

The Cambridge Introduction to
Charles Dickens

Charles Dickens became immensely popular early on in his career as a
novelist, and his appeal continues to grow with new editions prompted
by recent television and film adaptations, as well as large numbers
of students studying the Victorian novel. This lively and accessible
introduction to Dickens focuses on the extraordinary diversity of his
writing. Jon Mee discusses Dickens's novels, journalism and public
performances, the historical contexts and his influence on other writers.
In the process, five major themes emerge: Dickens the entertainer;
Dickens and language; Dickens and London; Dickens, gender, and
domesticity; and the question of adaptation, including Dickens's
adaptations of his own work. These interrelated concerns allow readers
to start making their own new connections between his famous and less
widely read works and to appreciate fully the sheer imaginative richness
of his writing, which particularly evokes the dizzying expansion of
nineteenth-century London.

Jon Mee is Professor of Romanticism Studies at the University of
Warwick. With Tom Keymer, he edited *The Cambridge Companion to
English Literature, 1740–1830* (2004).

Contents

Illustrations

Preface

Years ago now, when, like Magwitch, I arrived back in England from Australia, I was plunged into the experience of teaching Dickens at University College, Oxford. Unlike the returned transportee, I didn't come to serious harm beneath the grinding wheels of the paddle steamer, although it was something of a close call. Nor did I find myself confined in prison. Far from it, in fact, as the experience of encountering the novels afresh (I had not taught them in Australia) was to prove one of those painful pleasures that proliferate in Dickens. Painful because, like Matthew Pocket, I had become a tutorial 'grinder'. Trying to teach various combinations of the novels to individual students over the course of a single week could culminate in a final hazy Friday afternoon tutorial, where every character seemed to have crowded together in one huge canvas. Mrs Gamp and Mr Micawber, to name but two, may have turned up in more than one novel – sometimes, I'm afraid, together. The pleasure, of course, was in the sheer imaginative richness of the writing, and listening to undergraduates respond to it with such obvious enthusiasm. This book is conceived of as an 'introduction' to this wonderful diversity rather than a guide that painstakingly offers a commentary on each novel. Guides of that kind are numerous, and many of them are excellent, but I've attempted a more inductive approach by using five topics to open up the richness of the Dickens world, including the question of adaptation, something that started while Dickens was alive and to which Dickens himself contributed via public performances of his work. My aim has not been to consecrate great works, which they are by any measure, but to open them up to new pleasures in the experience of new readers, including you, I hope, dear reader. The five chapters focus on the issues that have always attracted me as a reader and teacher of Dickens. As a set of concerns, each has grown out of and relates back to the others, partly through associations that have often been unconscious to me, but which I hope are made more explicit here, and make sense to readers as you make connections for yourselves. As a consequence of this form of address to my subject (and to you), the aim is that the parts should not be detachable but that the book will have to be read whole as an introduction. It's been written with readability in mind, although I hope not at the expense of the seriousness of some of the issues it develops. I have written in a way that I still believe will be useful to students and general readers, but not in a way that allows you to read just one section, for instance, if you have an essay to write on *A Tale of Two Cities* (not, of course, that I can stop you using the index!). As a consequence of this more personal method, some novels are given more attention than others, especially perhaps *Oliver Twist, Dombey and Son, Bleak House, Great Expectations*, and *Our Mutual Friend*. I have not made these choices on the basis of canonicity, or 'greatness', or even popularity. The choices have been made on the basis of which seems best to enable me to say what I think needs to be said to introduce Dickens. Some readers may, for instance, find rather more of *Barnaby Rudge* than is often the case in books about Dickens. That instance grows out of the peculiar trajectory by which I have come to know and love Dickens, reflecting the fact that, as a professional academic, most of my work has been in the Romantic period rather than the Victorian. No doubt some readers and many experts will find this approach to result in a distortion of *their* Dickens. Even so, my hope is that these readers and experts will find something useful in these pages, even if they don't subscribe to the whole package.

The book is the product of those experiences teaching in Oxford. I am grateful to the undergraduates of University College, who, for ten years, put up with my grinding and sharpened my own wits in return. I also benefited from a series of American summer schools, most especially three sessions of the British School At Oxford (BSAO) under the benign direction of Mike Leslie. Students in all these contexts helped me immensely in understanding Dickens and questioning my own assumptions. My fellow faculty on the BSAO programme were a constant source of encouragement. I am also grateful to Judith Luna for giving me the opportunity to co-edit *Barnaby Rudge* for Oxford World's Classics, my first opportunity to explore my Dickens teaching in print, and to my co-editors Clive Hurst and Iain McCalman. Clive also very helpfully provided access to the Bodleian's holdings of the novels in their weekly or monthly parts. My relationship with Dickens was given an important fillip by co-convening the conference on *A Tale of Two Cities* and the French Revolution held at St Anne's College, Oxford, in July 2006. Colin Jones and Jo McDonagh made the job of running a conference and co-editing the resultant collection of essays an exercise in conviviality. The contributors to the volume considerably expanded the range of my knowledge on a series of fronts, especially, again, in relation to cinema and theatre adaptations. The sad death of one of the contributors, Sally Ledger, just before the collection was published was a terrible loss, not only personally but also for future Dickens scholarship. Academically, I gained greatly from being present at the workshop she hosted on Dickens and America at the 'Idea of America' conference held at the Institute of English Studies in June 2008. I am grateful to the convenors Ella Dzelainis and Ruth Livesey for inviting me to speak. I have also benefited from conversations about Dickens with Luisa Calè, David Goldie, Peter D. McDonald, and David Paroissien. David Fallon helped immensely with the final presentation of the manuscript. I am grateful for his advice and his enthusiasm. The final version of the typescript was prepared in the Humanities Research Centre of the Australian National University. Magwitch, in this adaptation, makes it back. I am grateful to the Director, Debjani Ganguly, for finding space for me, and to Leena Messina for all her help and support. Gillian Russell very kindly bought me a copy of Michael Slater's excellent biography almost as soon as it arrived in Canberra. Finally, Linda Bree has been a model of patient encouragement as an editor. Any mistakes in what follows, together with all its opinions, remain my own responsibility. Dickens always wished his readers to be companions but had to accept they would go their own ways. I publish this book with the hope that even you recalcitrant readers who disagree with what follows will still want to go on to read and re-read the novels.

Chronology

1812	Born Charles John Huffham Dickens in Portsmouth (7 February) to John and Elizabeth Dickens.
1817	Family moves to Chatham, near Rochester in Kent, where they stay for four years.
1821	Dickens begins education at the school of William Giles, a Baptist minister.
1822	John Dickens transferred to London. Family moves to 16 Bayham Street, Camden Town.
1824	Charles is sent to work at Warren's blacking factory, probably early in February. John Dickens imprisoned for debt in the Marshalsea Prison (20 February – 28 May).
1825	Attends Wellington House Academy on Hampstead Road for two years.
1827	Family evicted for non-payment of rates (March). Dickens leaves school in May and becomes a clerk at a firm of solicitors, Ellis and Blackmore in Gray's Inn.
1828–9	Learns shorthand and works as a freelance court reporter at Doctors' Commons.
1830	Falls in love with Maria Beadnell, daughter of a banker.
1831–4	Follows his father in starting work as a parliamentary reporter.
1832	Considers a career in acting but fails to keep his appointment for audition at Covent Garden Theatre through illness.
1833	Publishes first story, 'A Dinner at Poplar Walk', the first of several in the *Monthly Magazine*.
1834	Becomes reporter for the *Morning Chronicle*. Meets Catherine Hogarth (August). Publishes stories in various periodicals.
1836	Collects previously published stories into his first book, *Sketches by Boz*. Marries Catherine Hogarth (2 April). Serialization of *The Pickwick Papers* from 31 March. His burletta *The Strange Gentleman* opens at the St James's Theatre (29 September) followed

by the operetta *The Village Coquettes* (6 December). *Sketches by Boz*, Second Series, published at the end of the year. Resigns from the *Morning Chronicle* to become editor of *Bentley's Miscellany*.

1837 Charles Culliford Boz (Charley) Dickens, first of his ten children born (6 January). Death of Mary Hogarth (7 May). *Oliver Twist* serialized in *Bentley's* from February.

1838 Edits *Memoirs of Joseph Grimaldi*. First monthly part of *Nicholas Nickleby* published 31 March.

1839 Resigns editorship of *Bentley's Miscellany* (31 January).

1840 *The Old Curiosity Shop* serialized in *Master Humphrey's Clock* from late April.

1841 *Barnaby Rudge* serialized in *Master Humphrey's Clock* from 13 February.

1842 In the USA for the first half of the year. *American Notes* published.

1843 *Martin Chuzzlewit* published in monthly parts from January 1843. First of his annual Christmas stories, *A Christmas Carol*, published (19 December).

1844 Lives with his family in Italy for a year from July. *The Chimes* published (16 December).

1845 *The Cricket on the Hearth* published (20 December). Begins composition of the autobiographical fragment (*c.* 1845–8) finally published in Forster's *Life*.

1846 Edits the *Daily News* but resigns abruptly early in February. Family leaves in May to live part of the year in Switzerland and Paris. *Pictures from Italy* published (18 May). *Dombey and Son* published in monthly parts from October.

1848 *The Haunted Man* published (19 December).

1849 *David Copperfield* published in monthly parts from May.

1850 Founds and edits the weekly journal *Household Words* from March.

1851 Dickens family moves to Tavistock House (November).

1852 *Bleak House* serialized in monthly parts from March.

1854 *Hard Times* serialized in *Household Words* from April.

1855 Meets Maria Beadnell (now Mrs Winter) again. Lives in Paris (October 1855 – April 1856). *Little Dorrit* published in monthly parts from December 1855.

1856 Purchases house at Gad's Hill Place, near Rochester in Kent. Collaborates with Wilkie Collins on *The Frozen Deep*.

1857 Directs and acts in *The Frozen Deep* (January). Meets and falls in love with the actress Ellen Ternan.

1858	Gives his first professional public readings (April). Legal separation from Catherine (May). First provincial reading tour (August – November).
1859	Founds and edits the weekly *All the Year Round* from April. First number features the first part of *A Tale of Two Cities*.
1860	*Great Expectations* serialized in *All the Year Round* from December and succeeds in reviving its flagging sales.
1864	*Our Mutual Friend* published in monthly installments from the end of April.
1865	Staplehurst train wreck in Kent (9 June). Dickens injured but helps with injured and dying. Later has recurring nightmares about the crash.
1867	Final American reading tour (November 1867 – April 1868).
1870	Resumption of farewell readings in London (January). Audience with Queen Victoria (9 March). Begins serializing *The Mystery of Edwin Drood* (April). Dies at Gad's Hill on 9 June from a brain haemorrhage.

Abbreviations

Collins a	Philip Collins (ed.), *Charles Dickens: The Critical Heritage* (London and New York: Routledge, 1971)
Collins b	Philip Collins (ed.), *Charles Dickens: The Public Readings* (Oxford: Oxford University Press, 1975)
DSA	*Dickens Studies Annual: Essays on Victorian Fiction*
Forster	John Forster, *The Life of Charles Dickens*, 3 vols. (London: Chapman & Hall, 1872–4). New edition, with notes and index by J. W. T. Ley (London: Cecil Palmer, 1928)
J	Michael Slater and John Drew, eds., *The Dent Uniform Edition of Dickens' Journalism*, 4 vols. (London: Dent, 1994–2000)
L	*The Letters of Charles Dickens*, ed. Madeline House, Graham Storey, Kathleen Tillotson et al., 12 vols. (Oxford: Oxford University Press, 1965–2002)
Speeches	*Speeches of Charles Dickens*, ed. K. J. Fielding (Oxford: Clarendon Press, 1960)

References to these sources will be given in the main text. Quotations from the novels are taken from the Penguin paperback editions, published in London, and given in the text, sourced to volume (where relevant), chapter, and page(s) in the format '(1: 2, 3)', and with the following abbreviations:

BH	*Bleak House*, ed. with an introduction and notes by Nicola Bradbury. Preface by Terry Eagleton (2003)
BR	*Barnaby Rudge*, ed. with an introduction and notes by John Bowen (2003)
DC	*David Copperfield*, ed. with an introduction and notes by Jeremy Tambling (2004)
DS	*Dombey and Son*, ed. with an introduction and notes by Andrew Sanders (2002)
GE	*Great Expectations*, ed. with an introduction by David Trotter and notes by Charlotte Mitchell (2003)

LD	*Little Dorrit*, ed. with an introduction by Stephen Wall and notes by Helen Small (2003)
MC	*Martin Chuzzlewit*, ed. with an introduction and notes by Patricia Ingham (2004)
MED	*Mystery of Edwin Drood*, ed. with an introduction and notes by David Paroissien (2002)
NN	*Nicholas Nickleby*, ed. with an introduction and notes by Mark Ford (2003)
OCS	*The Old Curiosity Shop*, ed. with an introduction and notes by Norman Page (2003)
OMF	*Our Mutual Friend*, ed. with an introduction and notes by Adrian Poole (1997)
OT	*Oliver Twist*, ed. with an introduction and notes by Philip Horne (2003)
PI	*Pictures from Italy*, ed. with an introduction and notes by Kate Flint (2006)
PP	*The Pickwick Papers*, ed. with an introduction and notes by Mark Wormald (2003)
TTC	*A Tale of Two Cities*, ed. with an introduction and notes by Richard Maxwell (2003)

Chapter 1

Dickens the entertainer: 'People must be amuthed'

Charles Dickens was born in Portsmouth on 7 February 1812, into a world and into a family offering him little security. His mother was Elizabeth Dickens, née Barrow, the daughter of a naval paymaster found guilty of embezzling money from his employer two years before Charles was born. His father, John, was a clerk in the Navy Pay Office, originally in London but moved to be near Portsmouth's naval dockyard in 1810. Dickens was the second child born into a household that never stayed anywhere for very long. He never felt he had received the support and succour he deserved from either of his parents. Rapid transitions and stark contrasts were as much a part of his childhood as they are fundamental to his novels. In his early childhood, a series of different residences in Portsmouth was followed by removal back to London in 1814 when the Admiralty reorganized at the end of the Napoleonic War. This was the earliest contact with London for a novelist whose love and loathing for the great expanding metropolis was to define his fiction for many of his readers.

Initially at least, it was a relatively short-lived encounter between a writer and his inspiration, for only two years later the family then moved to be near the naval dockyards in Kent. Dickens memorably described this flat coastal landscape of indeterminate land and sea at the beginning of *Great Expectations*, when the soldiery hunt down the escaped convict Abel Magwitch across its dreary wastes. If the young hero Pip's imaginative life is profoundly shaped by those events on the Kent marshes, then it was there too, in the fast-changing world of the 1810s, as Britain emerged from nearly three decades of war with France, that Dickens seems to have made his first attempts at writing. Not for him the introspections of a diary or the creation of a fantasy world closed to others: Dickens, instead, with an emphasis on performance he was never to lose, began by directing plays for the family in the kitchen and performing songs standing on a table in a local pub. He told Mary Howitt in 1859 that he had been 'a great writer at 8 years old or so' and 'an actor and a speaker from a baby' (*L* 9: 119). Often to the dismay of literary friends such as his biographer John Forster, entertainment remained at the heart of the literary enterprise for him. Even after he had secured his reputation as 'the Inimitable', he adapted his own novels for public readings and, from 1858, took them out to perform himself to audiences in England, Ireland, Scotland, France, and the USA.[1]

When the Dickens family moved back to London in 1822, the financial difficulties that would continue to make problems for them were catching up with John Dickens. The most immediate result for the young Charles was being sent away from home to work at Warren's blacking factory. The firm manufactured boot polish in a warehouse by the side of the Thames. Not himself one of the urban poor or one of those thousands of economic migrants increasingly drawn to the city, this experience nevertheless seems to have given him a sharp sense of the uncertainty of life for those in the lower classes of the vibrant but harsh metropolis. Certainly the experience in the blacking factory, first written up in 'the autobiographical fragment' for Forster, reappears in one shape or another throughout his fiction, most directly in the closely autobiographical novel *David Copperfield* as the wine-bottling business of Murdstone and Grinby. More diffusely, the time at Warren's surely made its way into the horror registered in nearly all the novels at the degradation of mechanical work and, especially, in the reduction of children to mere cogs in a factory system interested only in production rather than the condition of its workers. Another event from his early life, equally calculated to undermine any sense of security in childhood, also reappears in different forms throughout the fiction: just two weeks after he started work at the factory, Dickens's father was arrested for debt.

In this period, debtors could be confined to prison by their creditors, at least until they began to pay them off. John Dickens, like Wilkins Micawber in *David Copperfield* and William Dorrit in *Little Dorrit*, was locked up in the Marshalsea Prison, and took his family with him, but not Charles, who lodged with family friends in Camden Town. *Little Dorrit* may represent Dickens's most extensive fictional transformation of these events, but, again, they play out more pervasively into a recurrent shame and anxiety of imprisonment across the novels. 'The stain of the prison', as Pip calls it in *Great Expectations* (3: 4, 353), extending sometimes to the sense of society itself as a huge prison, certainly informs the author's relish for the descriptions of the destruction of Newgate that provide the most vibrant passages in *Barnaby Rudge*.[2] Dickens wrote to Forster in September 1841 about his excited self-identification with the rioters while composing these scenes: 'I have let all the prisoners out of Newgate, burnt down Lord Mansfield's, and played the very devil. Another number will finish the fires, and help us on towards the end. I feel quite smoky when I am at work. I want elbow-room terribly' (*L* 2: 385). The nervous desire to burst out of confinement, even when the prison is the structure of his own novels, drives Dickens's fiction and provides much of its anarchic energy.

John Dickens stayed in prison for three months, after which the family's position improved – for a time – when he inherited money on his mother's death. The Admiralty then granted him a pension on the grounds of ill health in 1825, and he took up a second career as a parliamentary reporter, but he remained improvident – he was arrested again for debt in 1834 – and was a drain on his son for the rest of his life. He took Charles out of the factory when things improved and sent him back to school. From there, in 1827, Charles began work as a solicitor's clerk. Tedious though this work may have been, after office hours he began to experience the freedoms provided by the money in his pocket. He had enough confidence to volunteer his services to the newspapers, a booming sector in a print culture that seemed to be expanding exponentially in the 1820s and 1830s. Originally working as a shorthand court reporter, Dickens eventually joined the full-time staff of the *Morning Chronicle* in 1834. Around this period he fell in love with Maria Beadnell, a banker's daughter, but she had rejected his suit by 1833. Her attractions were later translated into Dora in *David Copperfield*. Dickens met her again in 1855, now Mrs Winter, an experience he rather cruelly adapted into the character of Flora Flinching in *Bleak House*.

In and around the world of the law courts and what we would now call the media in Fleet Street, there washed a bright and often lurid world of leisure and entertainment, nowhere more obviously than in the theatre, for which Dickens retained an enduring love. Always a show-off, he started to spend his income on clothes and began a reputation for flashiness. This relish for performance stayed an important part of Dickens's fiction. Serious 'literature' in the nineteenth century often struggled to adjust to this burgeoning world of commercial entertainments, but Dickens always approached it with relish. Novelists, despite the recent achievements of Jane Austen and Sir Walter Scott, were particularly sensitive about the issue, perhaps because they were still regarded as vulgar interlopers into the world of learning and letters. Dickens was not without anxieties of his own on this score, always being aware of the tenuous social and economic position of his background, but he never cut his writing off from what he called in one of his most brilliant essays 'the amusements of the people' (*J* 2: 179–85 and 193–201).

Dickens was and remains a great popular novelist. The judgement is not just a question of taste: his novels proved immensely successful with the new reading publics opened by the expansion of literacy through the nineteenth century, and continued to be so. By the end of the nineteenth century, he seems to have been the favourite author among schoolchildren of both sexes. Dickens penetrated deeply into popular consciousness from early on in his career as a novelist. He may have been outsold by writers such as G. M. Reynolds in the

1840s and 1850s, and even sometimes been suspicious of what he described to Forster as the 'many-headed' (*L* 2: 129), but more generally, like his friend Wilkie Collins, he remained optimistic about the potentiality lying within 'the Unknown Public' of 'three millions which lies right outside the pale of literary civilization'. Collins seems to have oriented *The Woman in White* (1860), the great mystery novel he published after 'The Unknown Public' (1858), towards the perceived taste for sensation in this new mass-reading audience. Dickens, especially in his decision to go directly before the public in his reading tours, which began in the year Collins published his essay, was equally drawn towards the new class of readers.[3]

The 1860s were a decade of debate about electoral reform and the extension of the franchise. The educated classes wished to include respectable members of the working classes in the new electorate, that is, those who could exercise their judgement but also recognize the authority of others over them. The public readings Dickens undertook from 1858 ought to be understood in this context. By attending the readings, the working classes were not only demonstrating their powers of discrimination but also perhaps acknowledging his authority over them. Not that this power was always in his control, either at his readings or in his novels. For decades after his death, Dickens remained available to working-class readers as a way of making sense of their experiences, often providing a language for those who embarked on writing themselves, even when they recognized he was far from offering any kind of realist window onto their lives.[4] If the greatness of Dickens has nearly always been acknowledged, then this 'popular' side of the equation has often made the recognition grudging. For William Makepeace Thackeray, a major competitor with Dickens for much of his life, as for many other contemporary commentators, including those who, like Thackeray, became his friends, there was always a touch of vulgarity about Dickens: vulgarity about the way he dressed, vulgarity about his manner of address to his audience. Henry James complained his characters were just a 'bundle of eccentricities, animated by no principle of nature whatever' (*Collins a*, 470). The result was 'a certain impression of charlatanism' (*Collins a*, 472). Too chatty, too close to his reader, too much of a confidential agent, too quick to turn the cheap trick: too much of everything, no restraint, no limit to what G. H. Lewes complained of as 'overflowing fun' (*Collins a*, 570). As one early biographer put it in 1858, worrying about the venture into public readings: 'Mr. Dickens, always fond of imagining a close, a very close, perhaps a too close, connexion between himself and his public, has, as we have seen, lifted the green curtain which generally hangs before an author's desk.'[5] The anxiety behind such judgements was whether Dickens was in control of his own effects and his audience's responses to them.

Dickens always practised the aesthetics of plenitude, where repetition is the soul of wit. Critics such as Lewes saw such prolixity as infantile: 'the reader of cultivated taste' reduced to the state of 'children at a play' (*Collins a*, 576). Certainly, Dickens regularly replays as farce what the reader has often only recently encountered as tragedy, a delight in repetition that refuses to leave things for the reader to contemplate from a single steady point of view. In *Oliver Twist*, for instance, the bloodstains that spatter the room where Sikes has murdered Nancy are revisited as grotesque comedy only a few pages later when the fleeing murderer encounters a commercial traveller peddling a universal stain remover:

> 'It's all bought up as fast as it can be made,' said the fellow. 'There are fourteen water-mills, six steam-engines, and a galvanic battery always a-working upon it, and they can't make it fast enough, though the men work so hard that they die off, and the widows is pensioned directly with twenty pound a-year for each of the children, and a premium of fifty for twins. One penny a square – two halfpence is all the same, and four farthings is received with joy. One penny a square.'   (*OT* 3: 10, 400)

Sikes snatches his hat from the salesman, who has threatened to use it to demonstrate the power of his product, and dashes from the scene, trying to escape from the memory of his dreadful deed. The comedy of the sales patter – with its own grotesque references to the victims of the factory system – creates a complexity of tone that is far from easy for the reader to categorize.

Recently, some critics have taken a positive attitude to Dickens the entertainer, arguing that this aspect of his writing, oriented towards a broad popular readership, is more democratic than any of his actual political principles ever were.[6] Perhaps, nowadays, we are apt, if anything, to underestimate the degree of social protest in Dickens's writing and its importance for his nineteenth-century reputation, but it is the entertainer who seems to have really grabbed his audience, even if we should be wary of assuming the two principles were always necessarily at odds. In one of the several direct addresses to his readers justifying his methods, Dickens identified the chiaroscuro technique in *Oliver Twist* with the rapid succession of light and dark in popular theatre: 'It is the custom on the stage, in all good, murderous melodramas, to present the tragic and the comic scenes in as regular alternation as the layers of red and white in a side of streaky, well-cured bacon' (*OT* 1: 17, 134). The implication of this defence is that melodrama is the genre best suited to the busy street life of the new urban world, discussed in Chapter 3 of this book, because it reproduces the welter of impressions, the bombardment of images that Dickens suggests is becoming part of everyday consciousness in the city:

> Such changes appear absurd; but they are not so unnatural. The transitions in real life from well-spread boards to death-beds, and from mourning weeds to holiday garments, are not a whit less startling, only there we are busy actors instead of passive lookers-on, which makes a vast difference; the actors in the mimic life of the theatre are blind to violent transitions and abrupt impulses of passion or feeling, which, presented before the eyes of mere spectators, are at once condemned as outrageous and preposterous. (*OT* 1: 17, 135)

Dickens was the kind of radical populist, not uncommon in nineteenth-century extra-parliamentary politics, who believed authority must always reside ultimately with the people. Certainly he was often impatient with Parliament, and his *Child's History of England* (1854) showed a hostility towards royalty, but if these attitudes – in terms of political belief – often seem to slip back into bourgeois liberalism, or even an outright hostility towards popular revolution, then in his writing there seems to be an open-door policy to just about every aspect of popular culture. From melodrama to nascent forms of visual culture such as the magic lantern, from fairy stories to popular songs and ballads, from courtroom dramas to recurrent mockery of the legal profession – all these are aspects of Dickens's writing attuned to popular taste.

Critics in the universities have often remained more ambivalent or even hostile to these aspects of Dickens, especially in the early fiction. Until a late conversion based rather puritanically upon the discovery of a moral centre in the later novels, especially *Hard Times*, the most influential of these was F. R. Leavis. He dismissed Dickens from *The Great Tradition* (1948) as merely 'a great entertainer'. Ardent admirers of Dickens, on the other hand, such as Edmund Wilson, have usually looked to the darker aspects of his work to justify their case, but the commitment to entertaining in Dickens is unrelenting, and central to that commitment is the fact that he is funny. Dickens first became known, and long remained admired, as a comic writer with *Sketches by Boz* (1836), a collection of newspaper and magazine pieces, and then in 1837 the huge popular success of his first novel *The Pickwick Papers*.[7] *The Pickwick Papers* produced a mania in the public, and many spin-offs, some authorized by Dickens, including tales reintroducing the main characters which Dickens worked into *Master Humphrey's Clock*, the weekly periodical he wrote and edited himself from 1840–1. Anecdotes abound, as they always do with Dickens's work, about the hunger to get hold of every installment of the book. John Forster retailed the story of a clergyman ministering to a sick man hearing him afterwards say: 'Well, thank God, *Pickwick* will be out in ten days any way!' (*Forster* 91). The book's origins were not necessarily so encouraging. They lay in a commission from the publishers Chapman & Hall to write a volume 'illustrative of manners and life in the Country to be published monthly' (*L* 1: 648). Illustration was key here, as the project was centred upon four woodcuts produced by the artist Robert Seymour, who had originally wanted to provide a series illustrating Cockney sporting life. If the series was conceived of as a description of Cockneys all at sea in the country, 'through their want of dexterity', as Dickens put it, then he managed to turn the project round to his own interests, typically expanding his canvas to include 'a freer range of English scenes and people' (*PP* 761) and in the process moving away from any condescending sense of Cockney inadequacy. When Seymour committed suicide soon after the project was launched, Dickens found himself with even more latitude to explore his own interests, although he still worked collaboratively with his illustrators, the Cruikshanks. Whereas other examples of this form of writing, such as *Life in London* (1820–1) by Pierce Egan, who also collaborated with the Cruikshanks, tend to condescend to the popular culture of the metropolis even as they celebrate it, Dickens offers a comic point of view that is more open to a diversity of perspectives on the world it describes. Egan's narrative is focused around three young gentlemen who descend, as it were, into London life, but are never seriously compromised by it. In Dickens, the middle-class Pickwick, a retired man of business, unlike the young Oxbridge gentlemen of Egan's fiction, is buffeted about by experience but also ultimately protected by the wit and wisdom of his Cockney manservant, Sam Weller, one of the greatest comic creations in English fiction.

Dickens later claimed that friends had warned him off publishing in numbers as a 'low, cheap form of publication' (*PP* 761). The whole thrust of *The Pickwick Papers* is towards upsetting such hierarchies of knowledge, despite the book beginning with a parody of a rambunctious club meeting, which might seem to suggest that learning belongs only in traditional places, not the 'Corresponding Society of the Pickwick Club'. Pickwick's pretensions to learning are parodied throughout, but scarcely from the stable perspectives of established forms of knowledge. In the book's many courtroom scenes, for instance, the law is revealed to be a place where truth seems open to infinite distortion. The funniest examples of legal legerdemain come in Pickwick's trial for breach of promise with the widow Mrs Bardell. Her lawyer, Sergeant Buzfuz, does all he can to read impropriety into Pickwick's innocent communications with his landlady:

> "Dear Mrs. B., I shall not be at home till to-morrow. Slow coach." And then follows this very remarkable expression – "Dont trouble yourself about the warming-pan." The warming-pan! Why, gentlemen, who *does* trouble himself about a warming-pan? When was the peace of mind of man or woman broken or disturbed by a warming-pan, which

is in itself a harmless, a useful, and I will add, gentlemen, a comforting article of domestic furniture? Why is Mrs Bardell so earnestly entreated not to agitate herself about this warming-pan, unless (as is no doubt the case) it is a mere cover for hidden fire – a mere substitute for some endearing word or promise, agreably [sic] to a preconcerted system of correspondence, artfully contrived by Pickwick with a view to his contemplated desertion, and which I am not in a condition to explain?   (*PP* 33, 454–5)

The world at large seems little better than the law courts when it comes to working out what is really going on. The book, to use one of the chapter titles, seems 'Too full of Adventure to be briefly described' (*PP* 16, 211). The mazy narrative of Pickwick's own adventures is constantly interrupted and obscured by interpolated anecdotes. Embarking on the task of reporting his observations on the country back to the club, 'that colossal-minded man' (*PP* 13, 172) Mr Pickwick soon encounters and is duped by a strolling actor, the noisy but empty Mr Jingle, whose bad behaviour, grounded in his ability to pretend to be what he is not, nearly leads one of Pickwick's fellows into a duel. Although we are quickly cleared of 'all Doubts (if any existed) of the Disinterestedness of Mr Jingle's Character' (*PP* 10, 129), *The Pickwick Papers* delights in his shape-changing variety, having him crop up in different guises throughout the episodic narrative. Only when Pickwick takes on Sam, a shoeshine who becomes his valet, does he tap a source of protean energy able to match Jingle's. Sam is a man of the world, but he looks upon it as a vast entertainment, made up, he tells Pickwick, of 'Sights, Sir … as 'ud penetrate your benevolent heart, and come out on the other side' (*PP* 16, 212). In fully theatrical manner, Sam even comments on the action in asides, a speech act, minor as it is, that contributes to the familiar relationship his character builds up with the reader. More generally, Sam provides a guide to enjoying the world while struggling with it. Part of the process is his awareness of profusion and opportunity in words and situations alike. He provides a distinctive form of colloquial commentary on the narrative, rarely as proverbial as it purports to be but always offering a wry perspective from below: 'Business first, pleasure arterwards, as King Richard the Third said ven he stabb'd t'other king in the Tower, afore he smothered the babbies' (*PP* 25, 329). Challenging but delighting the reader's expectations, then, Sam takes every opportunity to show the world is not always as it seems, not always amenable to only one point of view.

Of course, as with Sam's allusion to the murder of the babes in the Tower, this counter-vision often opens up a perspective much darker than Pickwick's irrepressible optimism. Although John Carey influentially argued that Dickensian humour ought to be understood as a defence against his awareness of the ugliness in the world, it is rarely as comforting as this diagnosis suggests.[8] For one thing, there is no orderly sequencing of darkness and light in the novels. Rather, there are frequently sudden changes of tone of the sort Dickens claimed he took from melodrama, and sometimes the reader finds their own laughter catching uneasily in the throat. Sometimes it is cruelly laughing *at* people, like the representation of a former sweetheart as Flora in *Little Dorrit*, or the depiction of the dwarf Miss Mowcher in *David Copperfield*, a picture he was forced to redraw in later installments of the novel after complaints. Comedy in Dickens is often anarchic, frequently disturbingly so. The set-piece comedy of the universal stain remover in *Oliver Twist* scarcely makes it any easier for the reader to come to terms with the death of Nancy. Rather, recognition of the comic virtuosity here creates a complex tension with the violent events witnessed only a few pages before. So, too, in *The Old Curiosity Shop*, the tics and rages of the Punch-like Quilp in pursuit of the innocent heroine are funny and monstrous at the same time, but they scarcely soften the discomfortingly lurid nature of his interest in Little Nell nor do much to distract from the disturbing question of the reader's own voyeuristic pleasure in it. In *Great Expectations*, where the opening chapters riff on the joke of Mrs Joe Gargery bringing up Pip 'by hand', a pun originally made in *Oliver Twist* (1: 2, 6) as a description of the unloving treatment visited upon the boys in the workhouse, the mixture of humour and violence is equally destabilizing. When Joe tells Pip that he and his mother had been 'hammered' by his drunken father, then the comic vagaries of his telling, including the death of his father by 'a purple leptic fit', only add to the complexity of tone (*GE* 1: 7, 46–7). 'The uncongenial and uncomfortable manner' with which Joe rubs his eyes with the round knob on the poker, while telling Pip this story, anticipates the discomfort of the reader caught between laughing at or crying with Joe as his 'blue eyes turned a little watery' (*GE* 1: 7, 47). The fact readers laugh with Dickens is scarcely a comforting factor, then, but proliferating points of view are part of the rollercoaster entertainment value of the Dickensian world of extreme effects, part of the sensationalism of his writing.

Victorian critics were increasingly worried about what was perceived as a growth of fleshliness in literary culture, a taste for being brought close up against material appetites and displaying the body all too readily, fuelled by the expansion of the newspaper press and its lurid interest in stories of violence and murder behind the façade of progress and respectability.[9] If *Sketches by Boz* and *The Pickwick Papers* offer a playful delight in humour, Dickens's other early novels catch a developing popular taste for shocks and awe, most obviously in Sikes's murderous rage at Nancy in *Oliver Twist*, heightened by the demand created by serial publication for cliffhanging cruxes and constant changes of tone. Even before the rise of the sensationalizing newspaper press, so-called 'Newgate novels', stories of crime and murder such as *Paul Clifford* (1830) and *Rookwood* (1834), written by his friends Edward Bulwer Lytton and Harrison Ainsworth respectively, had been among the popular literary successes of the 1820s and 1830s. Thackeray thought it 'quite wrong to avow such likings, and to be seen in such company', but their influence can be seen in the murder and mystery that runs through *Oliver Twist*, the tangles of whose plot Dickens struggles to control, and in the riot and violence of *Barnaby Rudge*, a novel that takes the reader back to one of the most violent episodes of eighteenth-century British history, the Gordon Riots of 1780.[10] In *Nicholas Nickleby* and *The Old Curiosity Shop* too the threat of violence to children, as in *Oliver Twist*, is used to awaken even further the emotional interest of the reader. Nor are these sensational effects just a matter of plotting. In one of the most famous and most disturbing scenes in Dickens's early fiction, the murder of Nancy, the rapid exchange of points of view, brilliantly captured in David Lean's 1948 film version, creates the sense of violence spiralling out of control. Nor is the reader ever safely outside of the scene, granted a stable place from which to judge Bill's rage, but pressed up close, struggling with Sikes, as he fights to free his arms from Nancy's pleading embrace; party to her fantasy of creating a life somewhere else together; privy to his brief flash of recognition of the future consequences of his actions; blinded with her as blood pours over her eyes; and then finally shielded from the dreadful deed even as the final blow is struck:

> The man struggled violently to release his arms, but those of the girl were clasped round his, and, tear her as he would, he could not tear them away.
>
> 'Bill,' cried the girl, striving to lay her head upon his breast, 'the gentleman, and that dear lady, told me to-night of a home in some foreign country, where I could end my days in solitude and peace. Let me see them again, and beg them on my knees to show the same mercy and goodness to you, and let us both leave this dreadful place, and far apart lead better lives, and forget how we have lived, except in prayers, and never see each other more. It is never too late to repent. They told me so – I feel it now – but we must have time – a little, little time!'
>
> The housebreaker freed one arm, and grasped his pistol. The certainty of immediate detection if he fired, flashed across his mind, even in the midst of his fury, and he beat it twice with all the force he could summon, upon the upturned face that almost touched his own.
>
> She staggered and fell, nearly blinded with the blood that rained down from a deep gash in her forehead, but raising herself with difficulty on her knees, drew from her bosom a white handkerchief –

Rose Maylie's own – and holding it up in her folded hands as high towards Heaven as her feeble strength would let her, breathed one prayer for mercy to her Maker.

It was a ghastly figure to look upon. The murderer staggering backward to the wall, and shutting out the sight with his hand, seized a heavy club and struck her down.   (*OT* 3: 9, 396–7)

The next chapter begins with light flooding through the city to illuminate the brutal murder. Dickens uses free indirect speech, the third-person narrator's voice registering Sikes's horror, when it gasps at '*such* flesh and *such* blood!' But Dickens does not spare the reader and moves into an extreme close-up that neither David Lean in his 1948 adaptation nor Roman Polanski in 2005 dared follow in its claustrophobic intensity:

> He struck a light, kindled a fire, and thrust the club into it. There was human hair upon the end which blazed and shrunk into a light cinder, and, caught by the air, whirled up the chimney. Even that frightened him, sturdy as he was; but he held the weapon till it broke, and then piled it on the coals to burn away, and smoulder into ashes.   (*OT* 3: 10, 397–8)

Here was the very thing critics of literary sensationalism found objectionable: human life reduced to blood and hair, the mere quivering flesh soon turned to ashes and dispersed. This perspective on life was not delivered from a safe distance but brought up close, exciting the reader, and seeming to encourage the pursuit of thrills that commentators often claimed led to the very kind of degraded lives exemplified in Sikes and Nancy.

The decades of the sensation novel proper are often thought of as the late 1850s and the 1860s, when the novels of Mary Elizabeth Braddon, Dickens's friend Wilkie Collins, and others were identified by alarmed reviewers as a new 'sensation school'.[11] Dickens contributed at the end of the decade by resurrecting the episode from *Oliver Twist* as one of his greatest public readings. Dickens approached 'Sikes and Nancy' with some trepidation lest it spark off hysteria in the audience. Performing this reading was often blamed for bringing on his death. His friends and managers begged him to withdraw it from his repertoire. If Dickens performed the part of Sikes with shocking vigour, then he is also reported to have entered into the screams and dying agonies of Nancy with the same degree of uncommon conviction. Looking on from the wings before the very last performance of the piece was to begin, he told Charles Kent, 'I shall tear myself to pieces.'[12] In his own novels of the 1860s, too, as well as the public performances, Dickens joined the sensation school that the melodrama and mystery of his earlier novels had to some extent anticipated. *Great Expectations, Our Mutual Friend* and *The Mystery of Edwin Drood* are all 'preaching to the nerves', as Henry Mansel, Dean of St Paul's, put it, and not just via their plots.[13] Through manipulation of point of view and narrative technique of the kind discussed more fully in my next chapter, the reader is brought in close to the action and given the experience of a dissolution of the self under the pressures of bodily sensations:

> 'I had drank some coffee, when to my sense of sight he began to swell immensely, and something urged me to rush at him. We had a struggle near the door. He got from me, through my not knowing where to strike, in the whirling round of the room, and the flashing of flames of fire between us. I dropped down. Lying helpless on the ground, I was turned over by a foot. I was dragged by the neck into a corner. I heard men speak together. I was turned over by other feet. I saw a figure like myself lying dressed in my clothes on a bed. What might have been, for anything I knew, a silence of days, weeks, months, years, was broken by a violent wrestling of men all over the room. The figure like myself was assailed, and my valise was in its hand. I was trodden upon and fallen over. I heard a noise of blows, and thought it was a wood-cutter cutting down a tree. I could not have said that my name was John Harmon – I could not have thought it – I didn't know it – but when I heard the blows, I thought of the wood-cutter and his axe, and had some dead idea that I was lying in a forest.   (*OMF* 2: 13, 362–3)

The abduction and drugging of an innocent victim, attempted murder, not to mention the setting in deepest Limehouse, are the very stuff of the sensation novel. Their narration here is further managed in such a way, with rapid changes of point of view between Harmon's description of his experiences from within himself and from outside himself looking on, that the reader is hurried out of any secure vantage point from which to judge:

> 'This is still correct? Still correct, with the exception that I cannot possibly express it to myself without using the word I. But it was not I. There was no such thing as I, within my knowledge.
>   'It was only after a downward slide through something like a tube, and then a great noise and a sparkling and crackling as of fires, that the consciousness came upon me, "This is John Harmon drowning! John Harmon, struggle for your life. John Harmon, call on Heaven and save yourself!" I think I cried it out aloud in a great agony, and then a heavy horrid unintelligible something vanished, and it was I who was struggling there alone in the water.   (*OMF* 2: 13, 363)

Such effects, quite apart from their savage content, were part of the sensation novel's warping of a position of secure judgement that critics such as Mansel feared would be replaced by the 'cravings of a diseased appetite'.[14]

If scenes which gave such a graphic view of low-life violence were suspected from early on by critics such as Thackeray of sacrificing the fully rounded viewpoint of serious literature to the pursuit of a debased audience's fleshly desires, then Dickens was – and is still – equally chastised for providing his readers with too much sentiment. Those who dislike Dickens tend still to see him as over-indulging in empty emotionalism, often compounding the offence by serving up sermons on right feeling to his readers. Sensationalism, sentimentalism, and sententiousness are closely related in his writing, part of the general tendency towards indulging a desire for more and more, whether it is for excitement, pathos, or indignation. Leaving aside the death of Little Nell in *The Old Curiosity Shop*, which famously drew crowds to the New York docks as they awaited the climatic installment, perhaps the scene that best exemplifies this aspect of Dickens's writing is the death of Jo in *Bleak House*, the itinerant crossing sweeper, who can neither read nor write, and who has never been taught the Lord's Prayer (the ultimate consolatory text for the good Christian reader):

> 'Stay, Jo! What now?'
> 'It's time for me to go to that there berryin ground, sir,' he returns with a wild look.
> 'Lie down, and tell me. What burying ground, Jo?'
> 'Where they laid him as wos wery good to me, wery good to me indeed, he wos. It's time fur me to go down to that there berryin ground, sir, and ask to be put along with him. I wants to go there and be berried. He used fur to say to me, "I am as poor as you today, Jo," he ses. I wants to tell him that I am as poor as him now, and have come there to be laid along with him.'
> 'Bye and bye, Jo. Bye and bye.'
> 'Ah! P'raps they wouldn't do it if I wos to go myself. But will you promise to have me took there, sir, and laid along with him?'
> 'I will, indeed.'
> 'Thankee, sir. Thankee, sir! They'll have to get the key of the gate afore they can take me in, for it's allus locked. And there's a step there, as I used fur to clean with my broom. – It's turned wery dark, sir. Is there any light a comin?'
> 'It is coming fast, Jo.'
> Fast. The cart is shaken all to pieces, and the rugged road is very near its end.
> 'Jo, my poor fellow!'
> 'I hear you, sir, in the dark, but I'm a gropin – a gropin – let me catch hold of your hand.'
> 'Jo, can you say what I say?'
> 'I'll say anythink as you say, sir, for I knows it's good.'

'OUR FATHER.'
'Our Father! – yes, that's wery good, sir.'
'WHICH ART IN HEAVEN.'
'Art in Heaven – is the light a comin, sir?'
'It is close at hand. HALLOWED BE THY NAME!'
'Hallowed be – thy – '
The light is come upon the dark benighted way. Dead!

(*BH* 47, 733–4)

This heartbreaking passage is pure Dickens in its emphasis on a child in distress, in its wringing of the last drop of pathos from the situation, and, equally, in the narrator's closing indignation at the institutions which have failed the boy: 'Dead, your Majesty. Dead, my lords and gentlemen. Dead, Right Reverends and Wrong Reverends of every order. Dead, men and women, born with Heavenly compassion in your hearts. And dying thus around us, every day' (*BH* 47, 734). If the last suggests a radical critique of society, which shadows the constant ratcheting up of the emotional stakes, then both coincide in their refusal of polite restraint, but neither easily resolves into the other. The exhortation and excitation of the reader are scarcely easy to translate into the discourse of politics or anything else: pathos and anger are part of a volatile interaction verging towards chaos. Introducing the Lord's Prayer at such a juncture may seem like over-egging an already sticky pudding, but the effect is scarcely one that affirms its sententious authority. The prayer lies unfinished, broken, and unable to comprehend the circumstances of the end of the chapter, inadequate to the needs of a situation designed to make the reader squirm. Like the law courts, the institutions of religion are unable to cope with what is happening in the world, which equally spills out beyond any idea of constancy of tone in the writing.

The Dickensian emphasis on popular entertainment might be regarded as primarily backward looking and nostalgic. Where the early novels represent the world of popular entertainment, it is often in terms of the vanishing traditions of the past, like the itinerant showmen of *The Old Curiosity Shop*, under threat from a new commercial society. From this perspective, Dickensian entertainment is associated with play and the plenitude of childhood, before the straitjacketing of conventional social roles. On a social level, it is part of his celebration of the values of community against the individualism of the new industrial society that Dickens associated with the beatific calculus of utilitarianism. Play is certainly a key value for Dickens: squeezed out of the child's world in *Oliver Twist*, apart from the dubious games taught by Fagin, parodied in Miss Havisham's exhortation that Pip should 'play, play, play!' in *Great Expectations* (1: 8, 59), and denied the young Harmon children by their miserly father in *Our Mutual Friend*. Compared with these perversions of spontaneity and freedom, traditional popular entertainments, such as the neglected maypole in *Barnaby Rudge*, often do seem to be associated with a golden past vanishing from a world increasingly governed by the work-time discipline of the machine. The hostility to utilitarianism and its reduction of 'the greatest happiness of the greatest number' to a mathematical formula is given its most focused expression in *Hard Times*. The appeals to the ideals of play and pleasure in that novel are primarily focused on Sleary's circus and the relief it offers from work-time discipline. *Hard Times* never aims to give a documentary account of a nineteenth-century circus, but even so Sleary's world is hardly one of nostalgia for amusements of times past. It is one of vibrant and even lurid colour associated with the sensational pleasures of a new commercial society:

> The clashing and banging band attached to the horse-riding establishment which had there set up its rest in a wooden pavilion, was in full bray. A flag, floating from the summit of the temple, proclaimed to mankind that it was 'Sleary's Horse-riding' which claimed their suffrages. Sleary himself, a stout modern statue with a money-box at its elbow, in an ecclesiastical niche of early Gothic architecture, took the money. Miss Josephine Sleary, as some very long and very narrow strips of printed bill announced, was then inaugurating the entertainments with her graceful equestrian Tyrolean flower-act. Among the other pleasing but always strictly moral wonders which must be seen to be believed, Signor Jupe was that afternoon to 'elucidate the diverting accomplishments of his highly trained performing dog Merrylegs.' (*HT* 1: 3, 17–18)

There's no doubt that the energy of the circus provides a structuring contrast with Gradgrind's utilitarianism throughout the novel, but it is not set apart from or above the world of business. At his very first appearance, Sleary has the moneybox at his elbow. If there is a visionary element to the representation of the circus in *Hard Times*, it is not one that in any simple way transcends the world of getting and spending.

More to the point, perhaps, the novels themselves seem to participate in the excitements of a new world of speed and colour, and Dickens himself was unapologetically interested in the commercial aspects of his own writing.[15] Oliver may dimly perceive a lost world of plenitude when he lies half asleep in the warmth of the Maylie domestic circle, perhaps taking him back to the fleeting moments at his mother's breast before she died, but the pleasures offered to the reader by the novel he inhabits are scarcely those of old-fashioned, pre-commercial community. Rapid transitions and intense verbal energy bring them closer to Victorian sensationalism than to village sports. Moreover, the plots of nearly all the novels require a new generation to break with the past. The Maypole Inn, named after the pre-eminent symbol of traditional rural past-times, is moribund in *Barnaby Rudge*, 'drowsy ... nodding in its sleep ... the bricks ... originally ... a deep dark red, but ... grown yellow and discoloured' (*BR* 1, 7). Joe Willet must rebel against the stultifying authority of his father, the pub's landlord, to find a place for himself in the wider world. Absent or default-ing parents are almost a precondition of the Dickens novel, one which means the plot is always forcing the action to step into the 'roaring streets', like Arthur and Amy at the end of *Little Dorrit* (2: 34, 859), where identities must be made in the throng even if against its current.

In this regard, Dickensian entertainment usually takes the form of the painful pleasures of modern life, the experience of a plenitude of possibilities mixed with feelings of dispersal and dismay, brilliantly captured in the inter-play between Silas Wegg and Mr Venus in *Our Mutual Friend*.[16] Perhaps no character in the entire history of the novel is quite as dispersed as Silas Wegg, who has to live with the fact of his own leg being for sale. The need to reconsti-tute himself, quite literally to buy back part of his own body, brings him close to distraction and provides the driving force in one of the novel's main plot lines. Venus's shop has what he wants, but such fulfilment seems perpetually out of Wegg's reach even when he actually manages to get his leg (or its bone) back. Nor is the situation exactly one of existential incompletion; there is also a powerful sense of social resentment in his need to gather himself together as a precondition for being a '*genteel* person' (my italics):

> 'Where am I?' asks Mr. Wegg.
> 'You're somewhere in the back shop across the yard, sir; and speaking quite candidly, I wish I'd never bought you of the Hospital Porter.'
> 'Now, look here, what did you give for me?'
> 'Well, ' replies Venus, blowing his tea: his head and face peering out of the darkness, over the smoke of it, as if he were modernizing the old original rise in his family: 'you were one of a warious lot, and I don't know.'
> Silas puts his point in the improved form of 'What will you take for me?'
> 'Well, ' replies Venus, still blowing his tea, 'I'm not prepared, at a moment's notice, to tell you, Mr. Wegg.'
> 'Come! According to your own account I'm not worth much, ' Wegg reasons persuasively.
> 'Not for miscellaneous working in, I grant you, Mr. Wegg; but you might turn out valuable yet, as a – ' here Mr. Venus takes a gulp of tea, so hot that it makes him choke, and sets his weak eyes watering; 'as a Monstrosity, if you'll excuse me.'

> Repressing an indignant look, indicative of anything but a disposition to excuse him, Silas pursues his point.
>
> 'I think you know me, Mr. Venus, and I think you know I never bargain.'
>
> Mr. Venus takes gulps of hot tea, shutting his eyes at every gulp, and opening them again in a spasmodic manner; but does not commit himself to assent.
>
> 'I have a prospect of getting on in life and elevating myself by my own independent exertions, ' says Wegg, feelingly, 'and I shouldn't like – I tell you openly I should *not* like – under such circumstances, to be what I may call dispersed, a part of me here, and a part of me there, but should wish to collect myself like a genteel person.'
>
> (*OMF* 1: 7, 88)

The absurdity of a man haggling over the value of his own leg is comic enough, but it is worked up in every detail by Dickens for more entertainment: Venus's reluctance to come to a market price for it; the pause to gulp and then be scalded by tea before he pronounces the word 'Monstrosity'; the idea of Wegg physically as well as socially elevating himself if he were to win back his lost limb.

And yet behind these inflections, each richly comic in itself, there is the knowledge that personhood is being dispersed into a market for spare parts: a dark shadow cast by the context of the shop (and the wider marketplace) in which the conversation takes place, stocked as it is by murky bits and pieces of bone and flesh drained of blood and vitality, the detritus of a supposedly glorious British Empire all jumbled together:

> Mr. Wegg, as an artful man who is sure of his supper by-and-bye, presses muffin on his host to soothe him into a compliant state of mind, or, as one might say, to grease his works. As the muffins disappear, little by little, the black shelves and nooks and corners begin to appear, and Mr. Wegg gradually acquires an imperfect notion that over against him on the chimney-piece is a Hindoo baby in a bottle, curved up with his big head tucked under him, as he would instantly throw a summersault if the bottle were large enough.   (*OMF* 1: 7, 84)

These descriptions offer to the reader the pleasures of the fairground and freak show, the baby in the bottle even threatening to turn into a tumbler as if he were part of Sleary's circus from *Hard Times*, but now in this gloomier late novel they are indicative of an anarchic world where life and death seem grotesquely jumbled, bodies coming back to life, and characters exhorted to 'Come up and be dead!' (*OMF* 2: 5, 280). The boundaries between what constitutes everyday life and what seems fantastic have dissolved into a Dickensian dreamland or, perhaps more accurately, a nightmare.

The 'Hindoo baby' implies Wegg's situation is part of a much wider global net of dispersal and loss, drawn from across a vast commercial empire, where, contrary to Podsnap's bigoted trumpeting of imperial glories, the human body is contained, commoditized, and put on display for sale. With each mouthful of sustenance taken by the living, as the muffins disappear little by little into the mouths of Venus and Wegg, so these dispersed and desiccated bodies tumble into their lines of vision, 'recalled to life', as Dickens put it in *A Tale of Two Cities*, another novel concerned with resurrection, but still trapped in limbo like many of the characters in *Our Mutual Friend*. They include Venus himself, who, at the top of his trade of putting together the 'human warious' (*OMF* 1: 7, 91), had at least seemed to exercise some control. The dark humour is given a final brilliant turn when it is realized even he suffers from a loss of 'heart':

> 'Mr. Wegg, not to name myself as a workman without an equal, I've gone on improving myself in my knowledge of Anatomy, till both by sight and by name I'm perfect. Mr. Wegg, if you was brought here loose in a bag to be articulated, I'd name your smallest bones blindfold equally with your largest, as fast as I could pick 'em out, and I'd sort 'em all, and sort your wertebrae, in a manner that would equally surprise and charm you.'
>
> 'Well, ' remarks Silas (though not quite so readily as last time), '*that* ain't a state of things to be low about. – Not for *you* to be low about, leastways.'
>
> 'Mr. Wegg, I know it ain't; Mr. Wegg, I know it ain't. But it's the heart that lowers me, it is the heart! Be so good as take and read that card out loud.'
>
> Silas receives one from his hand, which Venus takes from a wonderful litter in a drawer, and putting on his spectacles, reads:
>
> '"Mr. Venus,"'
>
> 'Yes. Go on.'
>
> '"Preserver of Animals and Birds,"'
>
> 'Yes. Go on.'
>
> '"Articulator of human bones."'
>
> 'That's it, ' with a groan. 'That's it! Mr. Wegg, I'm thirty-two, and a bachelor. Mr. Wegg, I love her. Mr. Wegg, she is worthy of being loved by a Potentate!' Here Silas is rather alarmed by Mr. Venus's springing to his feet in the hurry of his spirits, and haggardly confronting him with his hand on his coat collar; but Mr. Venus, begging pardon, sits down again, saying, with the calmness of despair, 'She objects to the business.'
>
> 'Does she know the profits of it?'
>
> 'She knows the profits of it, but she don't appreciate the art of it, and she objects to it. "I do not wish," she writes in her own

handwriting, "to regard myself, nor yet to be regarded, in that boney light." (*OMF* 1: 7, 89–90)

The very idea of a 'boney light' is the kind of ridiculously incoherent conjunction that provides a major source of humour in Dickens, but the collision of terms also throws into relief the tragedy of the vulnerable body whose suffering and joys provide the locus of the novel's entertainment.

Venus's technical skills as an articulator cannot help him with his 'heart'. This bleeding 'heart' – present as a real place, 'Bleeding Heart Yard,' in *Little Dorrit* – is the central metaphor in Dickens for the human being pitted against the desiccation of the grindstone of society. Venus can put things together, but articulation is not animation. The 'heart' is the home of the living body, which feels the sensations of horror, laughter, and sympathy. Platitudes of 'home sweet home' are never far away in Dickens, but they never find adequate expression, nor quite fit the situation. Even when he gets back his leg (or, at least, the bone), Silas Wegg finds he is dissatisfied with his 'whole' self. He too wants more. No one is ever quite the hero even of his or her own tale in this novel. The question of the relations between articulation and animation in the novels, whether living is just a matter of putting things together, turns out to be more complex than imagining relations in terms of a market can manage. Never far away from the thoughts of either the narrative voice or its characters in the novels, there is the continual struggle to find a language adequate to its needs, productive, if nothing else, of the delightful and anarchic excess of Dickens's writing.

Chapter 2

Dickens and language: 'What I meantersay'

Looking back on his childhood, Pip struggles, even with the benefit of hindsight, to find a word to fit the discomfiture caused by his experiences in Satis House: 'I cannot hit upon the right name for the smart – God knows what its name was' (*GE* 1: 8, 62). The sense of 'the smart without a name' (*GE* 1: 8, 63) runs through the novels, intensifying in the later ones, increasingly suggestive of a gap between the profuse linguistic creativity of Dickens himself, on the one hand, and the constant feeling that the right word still cannot be found, on the other. The world of the novels is increasingly one where the characters struggle to make sense of what happens to them, where the constituted authorities of the law courts and the police can't easily find out the truth, and where society itself threatens to collapse into the gaps between words, ideas, and things. Pip early on speaks of his 'dread of not being understood' (*GE* 1: 9, 65). This chapter looks at this dreadful unease, which intensifies in the later novels such as *Great Expectations*, but also shadows and perhaps even fuels the energies of the earlier ones, driving them forward in pursuit of a way of describing the worlds they are constantly bringing into new life. The 'old practice of hanging out a sign', as Dickens puts it in *Barnaby Rudge* (16, 138), never quite seems adequate to communicate the full story of what is being signified. So, for instance, in *Barnaby Rudge*, 'The Maypole' is not a sign of convivial life in the pub it names but an indication of the mismatch between a dead-end place, dominated by the dreary predictability of the landlord John Willet, and a world of future possibilities lying elsewhere, most especially in the bright lights of London.

Acts of naming are the most basic processes in language, and in the novels of Dickens they seem infinitely fertile. Those many arresting character names – for the minor figures as much as the heroes and heroines – are usually the most frequently remembered aspect of reading Dickens: Wackford Squeers, the Artful Dodger, Mr Micawber, Uriah Heep, the list goes on. Names often seem to give a directly allegorical impetus to the creation of meaning in the novels: Mr Bumble in *Oliver Twist*, Krook and Dedlock in *Bleak House*, or Mrs Coiler, 'snaky and fork-tongued' in *Great Expectations* (2: 4, 192), and even Mr Sloppy in *Our Mutual Friend* (named after the 'Sloppy night' on which he was found [*OMF* 1: 16, 200]). Yet Dickens was suspicious of the direct correspondences of allegory, and the contents of his novels never fit into such straitjacketed structures. The painting on Mr Tulkinghorn's ceiling in *Bleak House* serves as a warning in this regard: 'Allegory, in Roman helmet and celestial linen, sprawls among balustrades and pillars, flowers, clouds, and big-legged boys, and makes the head ache – as would seem to be Allegory's object always, more or less' (*BH* 10, 158). Even in cases where names seem obvious in their application, they can still give the reader if not a headache then at least pause for thought. The violence and misanthropy of Mr Bumble, especially early on in *Oliver Twist*, while he still holds the 'porochial' (*OT* 1: 2, 8) office of beadle, is something more vicious than mere bumbling. Sir Leicester Dedlock's character, eventually at least, unbuckles to show itself to be capable of a selfless love, despite the allegorical importance of his position within the novel as a retrograde aristocrat, part of the process by which the mobility of narrative point of view in the late novels provokes readers to rethink their own positions and their relations with others. Other names seem right in ways we cannot immediately put our fingers on: Uriah Heep, Pumblechook, Jaggers, and Podsnap are examples. These names are important to the reader's understanding of the characters, implying a cringing hypocrisy in the first, ridiculousness in the next, a sense of sharp threat in the third, part of his grinding nature, and possibly the pomposity of the last, but they depend on an ingrained sense of the association between sound and the generation of meaning. The relationship is not logical but depends on the kind of intuition that might be thought of as second nature. Often a source of delight in themselves, sometimes even entering the English language to name the qualities associated with the character in the novel (as with Podsnappery), they more generally add to the sense in the novels of a world not structured in terms of some rational system of nomenclature.

The other feature of naming which tends towards this kind of destabilization, whether comic or darkly threatening, is the proliferation of names for a single character, particularly the central characters of the novels. Even Oliver, notable for retaining an almost immutable aura of goodness around himself, starts as a mere 'item of mortality', acquires the name Twist out of the exigencies of alphabetical ordering (the limit of Mr Bumble's vaunted 'literary' dexterity [*OT* 1: 2, 10]), appears before a magistrate as Tom White, and then is restored to his real name of Leeford. Whether Oliver comes into his own name as part of a restoration of the natural order of things remains a question at the heart of the novel's exploration of relations between 'nature' and 'circumstance'. 'Nature' is a word that has to stand a great deal of pressure in *Oliver Twist*, as in all the novels. When Noah starts to cruelly torment Oliver after he takes his position in Sowerberry's firm of undertakers, the narrator observes:

> But, now that fortune had cast in his way a nameless orphan, at whom even the meanest could point the finger of scorn, he retorted on him with interest. This affords charming food for contemplation. It shows us what a beautiful thing human nature is, and how impartially the same amiable qualities are developed in the finest lord and the dirtiest charity-boy.   (*OT* 1: 5, 37)

The aspect of the novel concerned with social reform is committed to the idea that circumstance bends and distorts human nature: 'The cares, and sorrows, and hungerings of the world change them [faces] as they change hearts' (*OT* 2: 2, 192). But Oliver's character seems resistant to such pressures, and Rose Maylie, 'so mild and gentle, so pure and beautiful' (*OT* 2: 17, 235) is elevated above any of the pressures that might have been exerted by the 'stain' on her name, as its fragrant sweetness of 'rose' suggests, despite her own fear that it would be perpetuated in their blood if she were to have children (*OT* 2: 12, 290). Women's natures often prove superior to circumstances in the novels, it seems, a topic I'll return to in Chapter 4. The character of Nancy, 'something of the woman's original nature left in her still' (*OT* 3: 3, 332), presents a complex case. Caught in a struggle between this Dickensian idea of a female nature and the pressures of her upbringing in 'the alley and the gutter' (*OT* 3: 3, 334), she is able to save Oliver but not to save herself from a fate at the hands of Sikes she convinces herself she cannot escape: 'I am drawn back to him' (*OT* 3: 3, 337).

Dickens often catches up the issue of 'nature' in the question of naming, especially in the later novels, which much more explicitly foreground the slippery relationship between names and the identities they promise to stabilize. The classic instance is *Great Expectations*, which begins with a hero who is unable even to say his 'proper' name: 'My father's family name being Pirrip, and my christian name Philip, my infant tongue could make of both names nothing longer or more explicit than Pip. So, I called myself Pip, and came to be called Pip' (*GE* 1: 1, 3). Pip's name is explained in the immediate context of his orphan status, which leads him to create a sense of his parents from the shape of the words carved on their headstones:

> As I never saw my father or my mother, and never saw any likeness of either of them (for their days were long before the days of photographs), my first fancies regarding what they were like, were unreasonably derived from their tombstones. The shape of the letters on my father's, gave me an odd idea that he was a square, stout, dark man,

with curly black hair. From the character and turn of the inscription, "*Also Georgiana Wife of the Above*," I drew a childish conclusion that my mother was freckled and sickly.   (*GE* 1: 1, 3)

Reduced to tears by his situation, he is immediately confronted by the terrible sight of the escaped convict Magwitch, who seems to rear up at him from nowhere. For the majority of the novel represented as a Cain-like outcast, indeed a murderer, Magwitch turns out to bear the Christian name Abel: the brother who is murdered in the Bible, not the misdoer. Magwitch may also be more sinned against than sinning, the victim of a moral universe too complex for the law courts to name. Having already been 'sentenced ... and re-sentenced' (*GE* 3: 17, 457), Magwitch is told 'he must prepare himself to Die', a sentence in the linguistic sense as well as the legal that seems not properly to fit his case.

Placed in this world where given names seem incongruous, or not to fit as might have been expected, Pip has to make a name for himself and in the process takes on a series of names. Philip Pirrip becomes Pip, a seed to be grown, then to Estella and Miss Havisham, who will nurture the seed to their own ends, merely 'the common labouring-boy' (*GE* 1: 8, 60). Herbert Pocket calls him 'the prowling boy' (*GE* 2: 2, 175), then renames him Handel 'for a familiar name' (*GE* 2: 3, 179). Joe feels he ought to be called Mr Pip, as befits his social elevation, despite the unnameable unease this creates for him. The idea of Joe calling him Mr Pip might seem to signal the loss of his true identity, except that the novel asks whether the familiar name he has lost is one he could ever have kept. Pip is a seed whose final form is much more open to question than the organic metaphor might imply. He may be foolish to try to deny his past, but the novel scarcely seems to endorse any idea of staying in one's proper place. Going out into the world while keeping one's sense of self intact seems to be the problem set by this shifting name game. The question which begins *David Copperfield*, the most autobiographical of the novels, 'Whether I shall turn out to be the hero of my own life, or whether that station will be held by anybody else' (*DC* 1: 1, 1), is frequently a question of finding a name that fits. In *Our Mutual Friend*, John Harmon, the 'living-dead man' (*OMF* 2: 13, 367), goes through a similar process of renaming to Pip but with the metaphorical framework extended to include the language of resurrection and living death, appearing briefly as Julius Handford, who comes into the plot to identify a body, before changing into John Rokesmith, and then, after being suspected of his own murder, being revealed as the 'true' John Harmon. The novel ends not with an emphasis on the restoration of true identities but with Twemlow's unexpected rebellion against the 'voice of Society' (*OMF* 4: 17, 794) and its idea of what constitutes a 'gentleman'.

If *Our Mutual Friend* ends with an explicit challenge to accepted understandings of the key word 'gentleman', then it's a challenge constantly being issued to language by the sheer exuberance of Dickens's writing. When he writes of the 'peppercorny and farinaceous' atmosphere of Pumblechook's shop, there is a savouring of the collision between the clunky colloquial adjective and its Latinate neighbour. The wordplay is not coincidental to the novel. Pip, like the other seeds in Pumblechook's shop, wants 'to break out of those jails, and bloom' (*GE* 1: 8, 53). Essential to the Dickens grotesque is the way inanimate things seem to have their own life, while human beings become like animals or things.[1] Often this is communicated in the tiniest detail, like the boots of the doctor who tends to Oliver at Mr Brownlow's 'creaking in a very important and wealthy manner as he went down stairs' (*OT* 1: 12, 88) or, to go back to *Great Expectations*, Pumblechook's 'mouth like a fish' (*GE* 1: 4, 24). Wonderfully, Pip is changed into a 'connubial missile' (*GE* 1: 2, 9) launched by Mrs Joe at her husband. Often the matching of adjective and noun, as here, makes no sense from a strictly logical point of view, much to the chagrin of early critics of Dickens, but it is a necessary outcome of the demands Dickens makes on language to keep up with his sense of the 'universal struggle' (*GE* 1: 1, 3) of life in his novels. Adjectives or adjectival phrases are frequently built up into piles threatening to scatter in multiple directions or at least conveying rising intensity. Take the first description of Magwitch:

> A fearful man, all in coarse grey, with a great iron on his leg. A man with no hat, and with broken shoes, and with an old rag tied round his head. A man who had been soaked in water, and smothered in mud, and lamed by stones, and cut by flints, and stung by nettles, and torn by briars; who limped, and shivered, and glared and growled; and whose teeth chattered in his head as he seized me by the chin.   (*GE* 1: 1, 4)

The three sentences seem to gather pace, each dilating upon the other in Pip's panic. The list of past-perfect participles ('had been'), surmising what has happened to the convict before, then pivots around the 'who', before the sentence swings into another list of participles describing him now in front of Pip, limping, shivering, glaring, and growling, with his teeth chattering, before the sentence suddenly pitches into action around a finally discovered verb, 'seized', as he grabs the boy. Language is put through its paces in these devices, made to snap and crackle, as it does for Joe, in the struggle to get at what he 'meantersay'.

Zeugma or syllepsis is the device where the same word (verb or adjective) applies in different senses to two nouns in the same sentence.[2] In Dickens it often links together a literal and metaphorical sense as with the famous instance where Pickwick 'fell into the barrow, and fast asleep, simultaneously'

(*PP* 19, 254). In *Great Expectations*, Pip returns from church to find 'the table laid, and Mrs. Joe dressed' (1: 4, 24). The very next paragraph begins with another co-ordination of the literal and metaphorical: 'The time came, without bringing with it any relief to my feelings, and the company came' (*GE* 1: 4, 24). The delay between the mismatch only compounds the sense of time being out of joint for Pip. Whatever their local effects, co-ordinations of this uneven kind, whether strictly sylleptic or not, abound in the novels, giving the sense of a need to transgress conventional language in order to convey a world 'of limited means and unlimited infirmity' (*GE* 1: 6, 43), to give another sylleptic example from the same novel, which frustrates or exceeds the hopes and expectations of its inhabitants.

There is one instance in *Great Expectations* where, pursued by nightmares after Wemmick leaves him a note reading 'Don't go home', Pip's tortured mind turns on the structures of language itself and makes them jump through hoops:

> When at last I dozed, in sheer exhaustion of mind and body, it became a vast shadowy verb which I had to conjugate. Imperative mood, present tense: Do not thou go home, let him not go home, let us not go home, do not ye or you go home, let not them go home. Then, potentially: I may not and I cannot go home; and I might not, could not, would not, and should not go home, until I felt that I was going distracted, and rolled over on the pillow, and looked at the staring rounds upon the wall again. (*GE* 3: 6, 367–8)

Something of the same struggle with grammar and the conventional forms of speech goes on in everything Dickens wrote. In the final completed novel, *Our Mutual Friend*, Wegg's confidence that 'you couldn't show me the piece of English print, that I wouldn't be equal to collaring and throwing' (*OMF* 1: 5, 57) is outpaced by a linguistic inventiveness that continually surprises readerly expectations. The serial production of new Harmon wills, like the proliferation of Dickens's own word games, ultimately disproves Wegg's boast to be the novel's 'official expounder of mysteries' (*OMF* 1: 5, 61). Like Mr Venus's shop, where 'nothing is resolvable into anything distinct' (*OMF* 1: 7, 83), things slip and slide into other forms. Jenny Wren is 'a child – a dwarf – a girl – a something' (*OMF* 2: 1, 222). Pronouns like 'something' and 'anything' and 'someone' and 'anyone' echo across the novel, as if language itself has become exhausted by the energetic pursuit and can no longer supply a proper name to anything.

I've already hinted at the way different novels tend to emphasize particular clusters of words. The late novels, especially, are often governed by a presiding metaphor, usually given a literal as well as symbolic presence in the story. So there is the fog in *Bleak House*, which literally and metaphorically obscures the truth, or the prison in *Little Dorrit*, a novel in which everyone seems chained. Even the letters of the family name are bound by chains on the front covers of the monthly parts (see Figure 3.1). In Chapter 5 of *Hard Times*, Dickens (taking up the role of narrator or conductor) instructs his lexical orchestra: 'Let us strike the key-note, Coketown, before pursuing our tune' (*HT* 1: 5, 27). What follows establishes the tonal range of reds and blacks that dominate the novel, conveying the hellish world of industrialization and the factory system. Different novels take up different patterns of colouring. *Great Expectations* keys into the 'red' of Joe's forge, 'flinging a path of fire' (1: 11, 93), but also exploits the cloudy greys of mist and fog, the brown 'ooze' associated with Orlick, the yellowing white of Miss Havisham's dress, and so on. This patterning in the novels extends well beyond colour tones. Often it involves exploring the metaphorical manifestations of a particular word and its associations. In *Barnaby Rudge*, it is the 'emblem' (4, 39) of the yellow key hanging over the locksmith's shop that offers to unlock the mysteries of the novel but may equally remind us of how much is repressed and locked away. When later in the novel Haredale looks up at it 'in the hope that of its own accord it would unlock the mystery' (*BR* 27, 223), the mute emblem offers him no guidance. The sign hung out never explains the meaning of events as it promises to do.

Closer enquiry often reveals an amazing degree of repetition of particular clusters of words bound by association across the novels, with different novels giving them more or less emphasis. So, to revert to an example discussed in my previous chapter, the idea of Oliver being brought up 'by hand' receives a single mention, more or less in passing, in *Oliver Twist*, whereas in *Great Expectations* it is the defining phrase for Pip's relationship with Mrs Joe. 'Grinding' or 'milling' is a favourite trope for Dickens from early on. It is often embodied in literal machines, such as the railway engine in *Dombey and Son*, but is also a more diffuse metaphorical presence in the other novels. In *Oliver Twist* the narrator declares: 'Oh! if, when we oppress and grind our fellow-creatures, we bestowed but one thought on the dark evidences of human error' (2: 7, 241). The outburst would seem to link the metaphor to Isaiah 3:15: 'What mean ye that ye beat my people to pieces, and grind the faces of the poor?' The question hangs over all of the later novels, often with the grinding metaphor still in place. In *Bleak House*, for instance, the Chancery is figured as a huge mill into which human destinies are fed regardless of questions of justice. Krook delights in retailing the words used by the suicide Tom Jarndyce to describe the operations of Chancery: 'it's being ground to bits in a slow mill; it's being roasted at a slow fire; it's being stung to death by single bees; it's being drowned by drops; it's going mad by grains' (*BH* 5, 71). Even the most enthusiastic of the law's servants are bound to the mill. The deathly solicitor Mr Vholes explains to Esther that it is 'indispensable that the mill should be always going' (*BH* 37, 607).

Predictably enough, the idea of the inhuman machinery of the mill becomes a keynote of the industrial novel *Hard Times*. In a landscape dominated by satanic mills of a quite literal kind, the most obvious manifestation of the human machine comes in the character of Mr Gradgrind, but the centrality of the metaphor there should not obscure the fact that it operates across the fiction as a figure of exploitation and alienation in Victorian society as a whole rather than simply industrialization. In *A Tale of Two Cities*, one chapter is named after 'The Grindstone' that whets the blades of the blood-crazed revolutionaries, who in their turn are associated with the oppressive blade of the guillotine. That relationship may seem only too obvious a metaphor for the inhuman machine of the Revolution pitted against the members of the Manette family and their English friends, but the word cluster has already had a complex metaphorical trajectory in the novel by this stage. The sufferings of the French people under the *ancien régime* have already been described as 'a terrible grinding and re-grinding in the mill' (*TTC* 1: 5, 32), a phrase that associates the Revolution with the wrath of God. The same metaphorical cluster serves to capture injustices on the other side of the Channel, when Dickens describes the attorney-general eagerly rising in court to 'spin the rope, grind the axe, and hammer the nails into the scaffold' (*TTC* 2: 2, 67). Even Lorry describes himself working for Tellson's bank as part of 'an immense pecuniary Mangle' (*TTC* 1: 4, 26). Although it's often read as a typically English disparagement of the French revolutionary temper, *A Tale of Two Cities* applies its vocabulary of grinding exploitation to the established order of both of its two cities.

In the next novel Dickens published, *Great Expectations*, the same lexical cluster of grinding, milling, and screwing plays a more subtle metaphorical part, finding a fleshly analogue for its mechanical associations in Jaggers's constant washing of his hands. Washing his hands of the biblical injunction against grinding the faces of the poor, Jaggers seems a version of Pontius Pilate, the officer of the law avoiding his moral responsibilities, insisting, as he does constantly, that his role is only professional and not personal. In the professional capacity, he is quite capable of turning an entire courtroom into a mill he is grinding:

> Thieves and thief-takers hung in dread rapture on his words, and shrank when a hair of his eyebrows turned in their direction. Which side he was on, I couldn't make out, for he seemed to me to be grinding the whole place in a mill; I only know that when I stole out on tiptoe, he

> was not on the side of the bench; for, he was making the legs of the
> old gentleman who presided, quite convulsive under the table, by his
> denunciations of his conduct as the representative of British law and
> justice in that chair that day.   (*GE* 2: 6, 202)

Unlike his clerk, Wemmick, who copes with the alienation of city life by divid-
ing his home self and professional role into two separate personalities, almost
two separate bodies, one seeming to be made of wood, the other more human,
Jaggers operates like a great machine, working on Drummle over dinner 'to
screw discourse out of him' (*GE* 2: 7, 212). The Law itself proves an implacable
machine, unable to adjust its mechanism to take account of the complex case
of Magwitch, who is ground under its wheels, much as he goes down under the
literal wheels of the steamship before his capture. When Pip falls ill, victim to
his experiences in the city, he imagines his alienation from any proper self as
an industrial mill: 'I confounded impossible existences with my own identity
… I was a steel beam of a vast engine, clashing and whirling over a gulf, and yet
that I implored in my own person to have the engine stopped, and my part in it
hammered off' (*GE* 3: 18, 462). Typically, the mechanical metaphor has already
appeared in a lighter key, when Matthew Pocket is described as having 'taken up
the calling of a Grinder. After grinding a number of dull blades – of whom it was
remarkable that their fathers, when influential, were always going to help him to
preferment, but always forgot to do it when the blades had left the Grindstone –
he had wearied of that poor work and had come to London' (*GE* 2: 4, 191).

London itself often functions as a great machine grinding its inhabitants down
into dust. The idea is elaborated in *Our Mutual Friend*. There the action is dominated by the mounds of waste – human and otherwise – generated by the great
city. The 'money-mills' (*OMF* 3: 16, 589) of commercial society are continually
grinding in the background, given more local form in the 'regular flayers and
grinders' (*OMF* 3: 1, 423) of Pudsey & Co. The 'grinding torments' (*OMF* 3: 10,
533) Eugene inflicts upon Bradley Headstone help sustain the reader's uncertainty about him as a character. Forcing Headstone to shadow him through the
streets, feeding him into the huge machine of the city, Eugene is tacitly aligned
with the inhuman processes of exploitation that form the broader backdrop to
the novel as a whole. Indeed, strange as it may seem, the metaphor even makes a
connection between Eugene and the villain Wegg, who continually 'screws' himself down and threatens to 'grind' the nose of Noddy Boffin, but also refers back
to Headstone, who, when he proposes to Lizzie, is 'grinding his words slowly out,
as though they came from a rusty mill' (*OMF* 2: 11, 340). Little can be resolved
into anything distinct in a novel where everyone has it in them to screw down
their best self. Even here, however, there is a version of the metaphor in a lighter
key. The mangle turned by Mr Sloppy for Betty Higdon sustains life (like the

pastoral paper mill that gives work and refuge to Lizzie). His highest praise for his former mistress is to recognize her as 'a woman and a mother and a mangler in a million million' (*OMF* 3: 9, 508). So too in *Bleak House*, Charley the maid ends up marrying a miller but lives deep in the country, surrounded by streams and meadows, part of another pastoral idyll. These lexical systems never quite balance out into allegory. They seem always to remain capable of being flipped over to the other side of the equation.

Perhaps even more pervasive than the machine language of grinding, screwing, and milling across the novels is the vocabulary of a literal and metaphorical marking and staining. In *Oliver Twist*, it appears most graphically in the blood of Nancy spattered around their room when Bill Sikes bludgeons her to death: 'He washed himself and rubbed his clothes; there were spots that would not be removed, but he cut the pieces out, and burnt them. How those stains were dispersed about the room!' (*OT* 3: 10, 398). In the darkly comic passage that follows soon after this one, the word returns insistently, as we have seen, in the patter of the universal stain-remover salesman: 'Wine-stains, fruit-stains, beer-stains, water-stains, paint-stains, pitch-stains, mud-stains, blood-stains' (*OT* 3: 10, 400). The stark reiteration of the simple word 'stains' insists on a metaphorical meaning deeper than any chemical can clean, but the question of whether stains can be removed is an important one for the novel. Nancy's eyes pursue Sikes to his grave: he cannot avoid the consequences of his action, which stain his consciousness and eventually kill him, but elsewhere in the novel there are stains which seem capable of being cleansed. Rose Maylie will not accept Harry's proposal of marriage: 'there is a stain upon my name which the world visits on innocent heads; I will carry it into no blood but my own and the reproach shall rest alone on me' (*OT* 2: 13, 290). The liberal and reforming aspects of the novel often seem impatient with this kind of idea, as I've already suggested (see above p. 22). The critique of the Poor Law suggests that given the right conditions such disadvantages would be overcome. Rose's 'stain' is washed out by Harry's renunciation of more worldly values, but other stains seem uncannily persistent and work their way through the novel with the same haunting force with which Sikes is pursued by his crime.

Not long after his first meeting with Oliver, for instance, Brownlow feels there is 'something in that boy's face' (*OT* 1: 11, 80), a sense of a relationship that picks him out of the crowd of street boys he will have seen every day. Here the Gothic heritage of the novel may sit uneasily with its reformist aspects. The 'broad red mark' (*OT* 3: 8, 387) that stains Monks's neck, and helps bring him to justice, is the most obvious example, confirming his own superstitious conviction that bloodshed is 'always found out, and haunts a man besides!' (*OT* 2: 4, 214). Likewise, in *Barnaby Rudge* 'a smear of blood but half washed out' (5, 50) continues to haunt the title character with the dreadful sins of his father. 'There are ghosts and dreams abroad' (*BR* 46, 386), Barnaby's mother tells him, but the Gothic novel has always been concerned with what Virginia Woolf called 'the ghosts within us'.[3] Dickens's novels are rarely if ever concerned with the supernatural as such; however often characters are convinced they are haunted or have seen a ghost. More important is the sense that the human psyche is governed by powerful unconscious drives that evade rational control and description by conventional language, such as Oliver's 'vague and half-formed consciousness of having held such feelings long before' (*OT* 2: 9, 262). In *Barnaby Rudge*, Gabriel Varden sees in the face of Mary Rudge, despite knowing it from childhood, 'the faintest, palest shadow of some look, to which an instant of intense and most unutterable horror only could have been given birth' (5, 50). The look is 'the very one he seemed to know so well and yet had never seen before' (*BR* 5: 52). The sentence calls to mind Freud's idea of the *unheimlich*, usually translated as 'the uncanny'. Freud defined the concept as 'nothing new or alien, but something which is familiar and old-established in the mind and which has become alienated through the process of repression'.[4] Varden recognizes in Mary Rudge's face the traces of a past event that he has repressed and made himself forget, but the past is rarely laid aside so easily in Dickens. Things continually turn up unexpectedly, eerily calling to mind something that has disappeared, creating the sense of an unease, which the characters struggle to name. The very repetition of words, patterning themselves across the novels, often in unremarkable contexts, builds up the pervasive sense of an uncanny text haunted by itself.

The staining of the present and the future by the past is an important part of the claustrophobic atmosphere of the later novels. In *Great Expectations*, visiting Newgate prison with Wemmick, still unaware of the influence of his encounter with Magwitch, Pip notes:

> I consumed the whole time in thinking how strange it was that I should be encompassed by all this taint of prison and crime; that, in my childhood out on our lonely marshes on a winter evening I should have first encountered it; that, it should have reappeared on two occasions, starting out like a stain that was faded but not gone; that, it should in this new way pervade my fortune and advancement.   (*GE* 2: 14, 264)

Pip tries to remove the sense of taint from his relationship with Estella, but cannot. A few pages after he has made this sober reflection, the note is replayed in a lighter key when he takes up the newspaper stained with 'the foreign matter of coffee, pickles, fish sauces, gravy, melted butter, and wine' (*GE* 3: 4, 355). Shocked to find himself associated with the foreign matter of Magwitch, he dreams of 'a gentleman unknown ... weltering in blood', although he finds 'no red marks about' when he wakes (*GE* 3: 6, 367). Pip only achieves a kind of redemption when he accepts the patrimony of Magwitch's stained character in a scene played out in prison:

> With a last faint effort, which would have been powerless but for my yielding to it and assisting it, he raised my hand to his lips. Then, he gently let it sink upon his breast again, with his own hands lying on it. The placid look at the white ceiling came back, and passed away, and his head dropped quietly on his breast.   (*GE* 3: 17, 460)

Absolution is granted here not by the courts or the church, but from the lips of a convict and murderer.

Even this inversion does not exhaust the sense of the uncanny perseverance of the power of the past over the present. Originally Dickens resisted any idea of closure in his narration of a final, accidental encounter between Pip and Estella on the streets of London (*GE* 508–9), but he rewrote the meeting, under the influence of Bulwer Lytton, so it takes place on the more resonant grounds of Satis House and offers the prospect of Pip and Estella staying together. Even so, if the novel's final sentence seems to offer a resolution, it ends up only ambiguously emphasizing the negative 'shadow':

> I took her hand in mine, and we went out of the ruined place; and, as the morning mists had risen long ago when I first left the forge, so, the evening mists were rising now, and in all the broad expanse of tranquil light they showed to me, I saw the shadow of no parting from her.
>
> (*GE* 3: 20, 484)

Even as there seems the promise of 'no parting', the romantic closure is haunted by the returning 'shadow'. The contorted syntax itself speaks to the novel's sense of forces at work beyond the scope of any easy comprehension in conventional language. From 1862, Dickens changed the final sentence to the possibly less ambiguous 'I see no shadow of another parting from her' (*GE* 507n), as if he recognized he had not previously been able to clear his own conflicted feelings about the situation.

The same cluster of vocabulary associated with staining and marking recurs in the last completed novel, *Our Mutual Friend*, now extended into the pervasive thematics of waste and detritus in the novel. In the opening scene, the narrator draws attention to an unexplained stain that marks the bottom of the boat in which Lizzie Hexham and her father ply their ghastly trade:

> But, it happened now, that a slant of light from the setting sun glanced into the bottom of the boat, and, touching a rotten stain there which

> bore some resemblance to the outline of a muffled human form, col-
> oured it as though with diluted blood. This caught the girl's eye, and she
> shivered.   (*OMF* 1: 1, 14)

The climactic action of the previous novel, *Great Expectations*, had also taken place on the Thames. Despite Bill Barley's telescope for 'sweeping the river' (*GE* 3: 7, 377), its secrets are not easily delved. Pip is filled with 'dread' at the idea 'that it was flowing towards Magwitch, and that any black mark on its surface might be his pursuers, going swiftly, silently, and surely, to take him' (*GE* 3: 7, 381). Later, Magwitch himself ponders its impenetrable surface:

> we can no more see to the bottom of the next few hours, than we can
> see to the bottom of this river what I catches hold of. Nor yet we can't
> no more hold their tide than I can hold this. And it's run through my
> fingers and gone, you see!'   (*GE* 3: 15, 437)

From its very beginning *Our Mutual Friend* develops 'the great black river with its dreary shores' (1: 6, 77) into a powerful emblem, winding its way round the action, connecting its opening with the climactic deaths of Riderhood and Headstone. If in *Great Expectations* the Thames seems inscrutably stained with the past, in *Our Mutual Friend* it seems saturated with filth and corpses, at least two of the latter unaccountably springing back to life. Dredging the river for the detritus of society, the bodies of the murdered and desperate, Lizzie and her father's activities show Dickens taking the idea of the past's uncanny return in a new direction.

The theme of resurrection had been an important one in *A Tale of Two Cities*, where Sydney Carton is 'recalled to life' (the title of the novel's first book), and, in comic anticipation, Jerry Cruncher works as 'a Resurrection Man' (*TTC* 2: 14, 170), but in *Our Mutual Friend* the living and the dead seem to change places continually in a crazy dance of death. The river may be full of bodies, but, as Gaffer tells Lizzie, it has been her 'meat and drink' (*OMF* 1: 1, 15), providing the wood from which he made her cradle. Other 'amphibious human-creatures' seem to have 'some mysterious power of extracting a subsistence out of tidal water by looking at it' (*OMF* 1: 6, 80). John Harmon, thought dead, returns to life after immersion in it to claim his inheritance. More grotesquely, in one of those off-key Dickensian repetitions, Rogue Riderhood also recovers from drowning, resurrected on the table of a pub having been given up for dead. The living in the novel are surrounded by the bodies of the dead, most obviously in the ghastly community in Mr Venus's shop, whose inmates often appear to be more animated than the living: 'the whole stock seemed to be winking and blinking with both eyes' (*OMF* 3: 14, 563). Now the past does not simply 'stain' the present but insinuates itself into every possible aspect of the lives of the living as dust: 'Coal-dust, vegetable-dust, bone-dust, crockery dust, rough dust and sifted dust, – all manner of Dust' (*OMF* 1: 2, 24). Even Mr Venus's hair is 'dusty'. The river, full of bodies, returned to the dust from whence they came, winds ominously through the plot, finally claiming Riderhood and Bradley Headstone. The remains of life, reduced to 'the dust into which they were all resolving' (*OMF* 1: 15, 184), hem in the action in the form of Harmon's mounds, whose fate more or less determines the lives of the characters.

'Dust' may be a key to the novel of sorts, but many of its secrets still refuse to be unlocked. Often Dickens makes this point quite explicitly in the novels by using devices such as paralepsis that describe by acknowledging an inability to find the right words. Like various other aspects of Dickens's writing, including the haunting of the present by the past, it is typical of Gothic fiction, where the 'unutterable horror' of the supernatural frequently appears as what cannot be comprehended in sublunary language. There, as in Dickens, it often excites the reader by the threat of a danger that is not yet or may never be revealed, often conveying the sense of a supernatural world overwhelming ordinary comprehension, as it does in *Barnaby Rudge* when Varden is unable to describe what he sees in Mary's face. The device makes its way from the early fiction of Dickens into the sense of uncanny presences that escape description in *Great Expectations*. An extended example can be found in the brilliant opening of *Our Mutual Friend* with its description of Lizzie and her father in terms of what they are not:

> The figures in this boat were those of a strong man with ragged grizzled hair and a sun-browned face, and a dark girl of nineteen or twenty, sufficiently like him to be recognizable as his daughter. The girl rowed, pulling a pair of sculls very easily; the man, with the rudder-lines slack in his hands, and his hands loose in his waistband, kept an eager look out. He had no net, hook, or line, and he could not be a fisherman; his boat had no cushion for a sitter, no paint, no inscription, no appliance beyond a rusty boathook and a coil of rope, and he could not be a waterman; his boat was too crazy and too small to take in cargo for delivery, and he could not be a lighterman or river-carrier; there was no clue to what he looked for, but he looked for something, with a most intent and searching gaze. The tide, which had turned an hour before, was running down, and his eyes watched every little race and eddy in its broad sweep, as the boat made slight head-way against it, or drove stern foremost before it, according as he directed his daughter by a movement of his head. She watched his face as earnestly as he watched the river. But, in the intensity of her look there was a touch of dread or horror.   (*OMF* 1: 1, 13)

The refusal to tell the reader what they *are* seeing is matched by the scrutiny to which the characters subject each other. The emphasis on nouns and verbs of sight, 'looked', 'intent and searching gaze', 'his eyes', 'watched', and 'the intensity of her look', even in these few sentences increases the sense of experience resisting even the most intense investigation. Rogue Riderhood appears with his own 'squinting leer' (*OMF* 1: 1, 15) and in the final image of the chapter even the corpse Gaffer and Lizzie have in tow seems to be looking out through its dead eyes: 'the ripples passing over it were dreadfully like faint changes of expression on a sightless face' (*OMF* 1: 1, 17).

While the novels do cohere to some extent around the kind of recognizable linguistic patterns I've been describing, their language is scarcely homogenous. Tone and register are continually changing to provide a shimmering sea of different kinds of speech that plays across their surface. Characters are known not just by their names but by the way they speak. Indeed, idiolect seems more often to provide a reliable guide to character than nomenclature. From Sam Weller's Cockney patter onwards, much of the energy of the novels lies in their openness to different kinds of speech, especially those, as it were, from below: Peggotty, Micawber, Mrs Gamp, with her reiterated desire for 'half a pint of porter … brought reg'lar, and draw'd mild' (*MC* 25, 387), are all obvious examples. Relatively speaking, the earlier novels show a clearer line of demarcation between the narrative voice and the other voices it attempts to herd into shape. Each of the characters I've just listed is marked as a grotesque by the way they speak, distanced to an extent from the authorial point of view, although Sam Weller is something of an exception; functioning as he does as the locus of popular wisdom in *The Pickwick Papers*, his asides open up a connection to the reader beyond the mediation of the narrative voice.

The picture in the later novels is more complicated. The Russian critic Mikhail Bakhtin has had an important influence on Dickens criticism by pointing out the extent to which the narrative voice is constantly being refracted through the other kinds of speech, literary and otherwise, that circulate in society. He argues that each novel offers 'an encyclopedia of all strata and forms of literary language'.[5] These languages are not just represented by the idiolects of the characters as objects of the narration but come to inflect the narrative voice itself in 'double-voiced narration'. Thus, whether the novels are narrated in the first person, as in *David Copperfield* and *Great Expectations*, or in the third person, used in most of the other novels with the complicating exception of the double-narrative of *Bleak House*, the narrative voice takes on various registers and genres: the language of the law courts, of utilitarian analysis, of business, or of the sermon recur inside the voice of third-person narration. This shifting relationship within any particular language Bakhtin calls 'heteroglossia'. Dickens's later novels often break down the hierarchy of authority between the supposedly neutral third-person narrative voice and these other forms of speech, but even early novels such as *Oliver Twist* often make brilliant use of a double-voiced narration.

The opening pages of that novel are narrated in the pompous 'officialese' of the workhouse and its utilitarian commitment to measurement over feeling:

> Among other public buildings in the town of Mudfog, it boasts one of which is common to most towns great or small, to wit, a workhouse; and in this workhouse was born on a day and date which I need not trouble myself to repeat, inasmuch as it can be of no possible consequence to the reader, in this stage of the business at all events, the item of mortality whose name is prefixed to the head of this chapter. For a long time after it was ushered into this world of sorrow and trouble, by the parish surgeon, it remained a matter of considerable doubt whether the child would survive to bear any name at all; in which case it is somewhat more than probable that these memoirs would never have appeared, or, if they had, being comprised within a couple of pages, they would have possessed the inestimable merit of being the most concise and faithful specimen of biography extant in the literature of any age or country.   (*OT* 1: 1, 3)

The circumlocutions whereby the language of utilitarianism takes over the voice of the narrator provide an immediate parody of the attitude that thinks of children as 'items of mortality' and reduces life to 'the office of respiration' (*OT* 1: 1, 3). In *Our Mutual Friend*, it is the pomposity of Podsnappery that so often takes over the narrative, distancing the novel from its imperial self-confidence:

> As a so eminently respectable man, Mr. Podsnap was sensible of its being required of him to take Providence under his protection. Consequently he always knew exactly what Providence meant. Inferior and less respectable men might fall short of that mark, but Mr. Podsnap was always up to it. And it was very remarkable (and must have been very comfortable) that what Providence meant, was invariably what Mr. Podsnap meant.   (*OMF* 1: 11, 132)

'Eminently respectable', 'Providence', 'inferior and less respectable men', 'short of that mark' are all words and phrases from Podsnap's conceited and complacent manner of speech, rendered elsewhere, in his pompous veneration for the British Constitution, as direct or reported speech, or as here taken into the narrative voice. One consequence of the prevalence of this kind of narrative technique is that language is revealed not as a static monolith but as a shifting sea of different forms all gaining their identities in relation to each other.

This kind of double-voiced narration is a subset of free indirect speech, a device more often associated with the merging of a character's language – and, therefore, their point of view – with the narrative voice's perspective. Bakhtin's analysis emphasizes the exaggerated comic distancing achieved by these effects, but they can also be used with subtlety, often without the reader becoming aware of what is happening – as they are in Jane Austen's fiction – to give the reader a particular character's perspective (even if momentarily). An example of such a fleeting effect comes at the death of Betty Higdon, where her encounter with Lizzie is rendered from her point of view, as becomes abundantly clear once the pronoun 'me' appears directly in the third-person narrative: 'It is the face of a woman, shaded by a quantity of rich dark hair. It is the earnest face of a woman who is young and handsome. But all is over with me on earth, and this must be an Angel' (*OMF* 3: 8, 505). If irony is the most obvious effect of such techniques, then here and elsewhere it can be used to facilitate the changes of perspective and tone typical of the Dickensian style. Unlike Austen's novels, where these effects often work to covertly build up our sympathies with the heroine, in Dickens such shifts of perspective distribute sympathy in complicating ways, not necessarily finally endorsed by the novel. So, for instance, as Matthew Bevis has pointed out, at the end of *Bleak House*, Sir Leicester's aristocratic manner of speaking, which has thus far been satirized when mimicked, is now allowed dignity through its incorporation into the narrative voice:

> His noble earnestness, his fidelity, his gallant shielding of her, his
> generous conquest of his own wrong and his own pride for her sake,
> are simply honourable, manly, and true. Nothing less worthy can be
> seen through the lustre of such qualities in the commonest mechanic,
> nothing less worthy can be seen in the best-born gentleman. In such a
> light both aspire alike, both rise alike, both children of the dust shine
> equally.   (*BH* 58, 895)

Without losing its sense that Sir Leicester's antediluvian Toryism has played a part in his own downfall, now he is broken and fallen the language of 'noble earnestness', 'fidelity', and 'gallant shielding' is released from satire for reconsideration by the reader.[6]

'Focalization' is the term often used in narrative theory for the way particular characters become the organizing centres for particular events (if not the entire point of view of a novel). These effects are not always produced by the kind of linguistic processes described by Bakhtin or those identified as free indirect speech. They are sometimes the products of the kind of visual effects that have made the novels so attractive to film makers (see Chapter 5).

An example – looking forward to the issue of the visual nature of Dickens's imagination – is the account of Fagin in the dock towards the end of *Oliver Twist*, where the reader is slowly brought to look out at the court from his point of view as if his eyes were a camera:

> He stood there, in all this glare of living light, with one hand resting on the wooden slab before him, the other held to his ear, and his head thrust forward to enable him to catch with greater distinctness every word that fell from the presiding judge, who was delivering his charge to the jury. At times he turned his eyes sharply upon them to observe the effect of the slightest feather-weight in his favour; and when the points against him were stated with terrible distinctness, looked towards his counsel in mute appeal that he would even then urge something in his behalf. Beyond these manifestations of anxiety, he stirred not hand or foot. He had scarcely moved since the trial began; and now that the judge ceased to speak, he still remained in the same strained attitude of close attention, with his gaze bent on him as though he listened still.   (*OT* 3: 14, 441)

The chapter opens with a description of the 'eager eyes' in a courtroom 'all bright with beaming eyes' looking *at* Fagin, but then we see with his 'eyes … observe … looking towards … gaze bent … looking round … he could see the people rising above each other to see his face.' 'All this he saw', we are told, 'in one bewildered glance' (*OT* 3: 14, 441) as if the passage were a single panning shot from Fagin's point of view. The virtuoso change of perspective in this one scene is far from overthrowing the sympathies of a novel whose narrative voice tends to reproduce an unthinking anti-Semitism in its descriptions of Fagin as 'the Jew', as Dickens himself later conceded (and tried to make amends for in the representation of Mr Riah in *Our Mutual Friend*). The question of Fagin's position is not elaborated into any consistent authorial take on his society in *Oliver Twist*, but the passage makes the reader more aware of the novel's contradictions in this regard. Specifically discussing the issue of heteroglossia in the novel, Roger Fowler makes the point well: 'the stylistic polyphony is provocative and creative, compelling the reader to grapple uneasily with the tangle of issues that Dickens problematizes.'[7]

Fowler makes another important point with regard to Bakhtin's ideas on polyphony, that is, the *nature* of the relation of the linguistic variety to the authorial voice. If grotesque characters, such as, for instance, Peggotty or Mrs Gamp, are organized in a hierarchy under the authority of the narrative voice *by* the very grotesque comedy of their speech, then diversity does not necessarily challenge the idea of a single authoritative point of view. If such speech is only an object of satire in free indirect speech, then the authority of the narrative voice remains in place. I've already suggested a few examples indicating that satire is not the only effect achieved by Dickens's use of free indirect speech, but what is the nature of the narrative voice itself? Does it have a consistent and authoritative tone and register? Quite apart from its refraction through the styles of the characters in the novel and other forms of social speech, the authorial voice does address the reader directly, often presenting itself in terms of a confidential entertainer, 'Mr Pickwick's Stage-Manager' (*PP* 758) as he put it in *The Pickwick Papers*, offering the reader a knowing nod and wink towards the shared suspension of disbelief as he works his magic. In *Dombey and Son*, narrating the sombre last scene between Edith and her mother, Dickens still speaks like a showman closing the drapes over a tableau mordant: 'Draw the rose-coloured curtains. There is something else upon its flight besides the wind and clouds. Draw the rose-coloured curtains close!' (*DS* 41, 635). Serialization – the publishing format Dickens persisted with for thirty-five years, by choice, long after most of his competitors stopped – added to the sense of Dickens as a travelling entertainer, albeit a familiar one, bringing news of friends and acquaintances. In its obituary for Dickens, *The Illustrated London News* wrote of

> the experience of this immediate personal companionship … as if we received a letter or a visit, at regular intervals, from a kindly observant gossip … there was no assumption in general, of having a complete and finished history to deliver; he came at fixed periods merely to report on what he had perceived since his last budget was opened for us.[8]

In the preface to the first edition of *Nicholas Nickleby*, Dickens compared himself to an eighteenth-century periodical essayist, delivering himself with 'the freedom of intimacy and the cordiality of friendship', imagining that 'on the first of next month [the reader] may miss his company at the accustomed time as something which used to be expected with pleasure' (*NN* 5).

Although readers were and are likely to think of the voice of the third-person narrator as Dickens 'himself' speaking to them, it often adopts this self-consciously chatty and theatrical manner. Take the following intervention in the narrative of *The Old Curiosity Shop*:

> As the course of this tale requires that we should become acquainted, somewhere hereabouts, with a few particulars connected with the domestic economy of Mr Sampson Brass, and as a more convenient place than the present is not likely to occur for that purpose, the historian takes the friendly reader by the hand, and springing with him into the air, and cleaving the same at a greater rate than ever Don Cleophas Leandro Perez Zambullo and his familiar travelled through that pleasant region in company, alights with him upon the pavement of Bevis Marks.   (*OCS* 33, 250)

In an influential discussion of the technique, Wayne Booth criticized this passage as tedious by-play waylaying the reader from the important business of the plot going forward, but, as he acknowledged himself, there is every indication that the reader of the Victorian novel took it as part of the entertainment, precisely like the commentary of a showman drawing back the curtain, especially in a novel that is a form of Punch and Judy, with Quilp as a particularly monstrous Punch.[9]

Set-piece interventions of this sort are actually rather less frequent in Dickens than is often supposed. Where they do occur, especially in the later novels, they don't necessarily resolve into a distinct point of view on the action for the reader. In the murky opening of *Our Mutual Friend*, for instance, Dickens seems to draw back the curtain for us, but also seems to share the position of the audience (on the banks of the Thames, it seems), straining their eyes to see what the 'figures in this boat' are doing. Here the narrative voice seems both to have arranged the scene for an audience to view and to be unable to remove (indeed, possibly even to share in) a sense of uncertainty:

> In these times of ours, though concerning the exact year there is no need to be precise, a boat of dirty and disreputable appearance, with two figures in it, floated on the Thames, between Southwark Bridge which is of iron, and London Bridge which is of stone, as an autumn evening was closing in.   (*OMF* 1: 1, 13)

The specificity of 'iron' and 'stone' seem only to mock the idea of an omniscient narrator: here he knows irrelevant details, but nothing that is important to explaining what is going on in the scene presented. Similarly, even in the first-person narrative of *Great Expectations*, despite the hindsight with which Pip tells his story, he never quite seems able to name the unutterable horror that haunts him. Although after Magwitch's revelation that he is the author of Pip's newfound wealth, we might expect the situation to be clarified, the narrative voice continues to tell us of its sense of confusion, and, as we have seen, the ending scarcely affirms the idea of a stable point of view from which the story is told. The reader does not know absolutely if the Pip who tells the story is now with Estella or not.

Dickens supplements authorial interventions that hail the reader with representations of reading within the text. Garrett Stewart regards both these processes as forms of 'conscription', which position the reader in particular ways in relation to the novel, and the society it depicts.[10] Too strong a version of this thesis risks understating the instability and obscurity of the narrative point of view I've just been outlining. In *Our Mutual Friend*, one of the main plot lines centres on Noddy Boffin's recruitment of Silas Wegg as a 'literary man' to read to him. The situation would seem to be a prime example of the readers being offered a parallel to their own position. Taking a suspicious view of the narrative designs on the reader, this scene may perhaps operate to affirm the superiority of the literary reader of the novel itself, unlike Boffin in no need of a one-legged ballad seller to mediate the experience. What this suggestion may underestimate is the extent to which Dickens knew his novels were read aloud or recited in public and private venues. The idea that Dickens was read aloud to the family group at the hearth was certainly a widespread image of his reception while he lived. Before he turned professional, Dickens first read in public in 1853 to raise funds for the new Birmingham and Midland Institute, a project – 'educational of the feelings as well as of the reason' – oriented towards popular education and entertainment and typically encouraging 'the inquiring eye' (*Speeches* 167, 160).[11] By becoming a performer of his own texts at public readings, Dickens might be taken to have accepted the dispersal of his texts into a larger literary public, although even at these readings he was still inclined to address his audiences in terms of a small, intimate circle of friends.

His own friends were ambivalent about the populist aspects of Dickensian address. Men such as John Forster were comfortable leisured readers, gentlemen not unlike Eugene Wrayburn and Mortimer Lightwood in *Our Mutual Friend*, who show a marked concern with the varieties of reading and readers operating in their society. Eugene and Mortimer's first encounter with the self-educated Charley Hexham, for instance, includes a lot of condescending joking about his gauche application of biblical texts he has read in school (*OMF* 1: 3, 28–9). Later, Eugene's confident social superiority allows him to presume to educate Lizzie Hexham, perhaps to make her worthy of becoming his mistress, but certainly to the fury of the self-made man Bradley Headstone who has had to struggle to make himself into an educated reader. Mortimer, for his part, is so secure with the conventions of literary reading that he can joke upon the device of novelists addressing their readers: 'We must now return, as the novelists say, and as we all wish they wouldn't, to the man from Somewhere' (*OMF* 1: 2, 25). Finally, in an extraordinary digression, Eugene embarks on a skit on the many different ideas of reading circulating in society:

> You charm me, Mortimer, with your reading of my weaknesses. (By-the-by, that very word, Reading, in its critical use, always charms me. An actress's Reading of a chambermaid, a dancer's Reading of a hornpipe, a singer's Reading of a song, a marine Painter's Reading of the sea, the kettle-drum's Reading of an instrumental passage, are phrases ever youthful and delightful.) I was mentioning your perception of my

weaknesses. I own to the weakness of objecting to occupy a ludicrous position, and therefore I transfer the position to the scouts.

(*OMF* 3: 10, 532)

Quite what the reader is to make of the digression in this particular place is difficult to say, but it scarcely affirms the idea of a normative literary practice in contradistinction to those forms listed, not least because Eugene's 'weaknesses', which Mortimer struggles to read, remain inscrutable to the reader of the novel until the very end.

The idea of a mystery that has to be unravelled was an important motif in the novels from *Barnaby Rudge* and *Oliver* onwards. Increasingly the texts remain inscrutable. Even after the mystery has been solved in *Bleak House*, for instance, there seems some excess, beyond the putting together of events, which keeps things in a fog. What the novel reveals to its readers is the difficulty of interpretation, of making sense of the world it describes. When the will is finally resolved at the very end of the novel, despite the many human sacrifices made to its interpretation, the authentic version turns out to have no value. Beyond this central example of reading, others proliferate in a novel obsessed with making sense of what one chapter title calls 'Signs and Tokens'. Krook's shop is full of documents, but he cannot read them, and once understanding starts to dawn, as he dimly makes out the shapes of the letters, he is consumed by spontaneous combustion. Making sense of things brings destruction rather than illumination. Caddy Jellyby is enslaved by the process of writing letters that are supposed, by her mother, to be bringing enlightenment to what she presumes to be the dark places of the earth. Richard is destroyed once the case of Jarndyce versus Jarndyce is resolved. Miss Flite has been reduced to madness by the case full of documents she carries in her reticule. The love letters of Lady Dedlock destroy her when they come to light. The reader has to make sense of all these dispersed documents. The task is exhausting and even unrewarding, especially if the pleasure of revelation is understood in terms of the emergence of a final truth. Reading is a more painful pleasure here. The more one uncovers, the more seemingly productive the engagement with the text, then the more truth seems to recede from the grasp of the characters in the novel and the more illumination seems to evade the reader outside it.

Appropriately, given its investment in the complications of finding the truth, *Bleak House* has the most complicated form of narration of any of the novels, divided as it is between two voices: the omniscient present-tense narrator, on the one hand, and, on the other, Esther Summerson, who gives her story in first-person past-tense narration to an unnamed correspondent. The two voices may collaborate as Esther describes her story as her 'portion', implying she knows she is sharing, but the relationship is never made clear. Is her correspondent the other narrator? The two different voices offer two very different ways of seeing the world. Esther is coy and uncertain, given to seeing things in terms of a providential pattern emerging out of events, but perhaps she is also suspected by the reader as disingenuous in her professions of humility and self-abnegation. The world recorded by the other voice seems much more disenchanted. It sees London engulfed by foggy mist, no further on than in prehistoric times. If the novel ends with Esther's happy marriage to Woodhouse, John Jarndyce stepping aside from what many readers experience as an uncomfortable engagement, then the mismatch between her worldview and that of the other narrative voice seems unresolved. However many truths have come to light by the end of the book, it concludes with Esther as uncertain as ever about her attractions:

> 'My dear Dame Durden,' said Allan, drawing my arm through his, 'do you ever look in the glass?'
> 'You know I do; you see me do it.'
> 'And don't you know that you are prettier than you ever were?'
> 'I did not know that; I am not certain that I know it now. But I know that my dearest little pets are very pretty, and that my darling is very beautiful, and that my husband is very handsome, and that my guardian has the brightest and most benevolent face that ever was seen; and that they can very well do without much beauty in me – even supposing – .
>
> (*BH* 67, 989)

Suppositions are more usually the beginning rather than the end of a story. Here, in an unfinished sentence, the 'supposing' points to the problem of closure in Dickens, the impossibility of a final word, whose place is taken in this sentence by a mark of punctuation. Such a sense of multiplying contradictions, of a world where tokens and signs do not yield up their meanings, is hardly surprising given the rapidly changing times in which Dickens lived and wrote. Possibly influenced by *Bleak House*, Wilkie Collins in *The Woman in White* (1859–60) later experimented with collaborative narratives that also gave a sense of a story that evaded any idea of final truth. Nowhere was changing more or faster than London, the fog-blurred focus of much of *Bleak House*, the centre of the economy of circulation and dispersal throughout the novels, the city that provides the content that Dickens continually strives to narrate. And it is to London that my next chapter turns in an attempt to account for its countless appearances in the novels.

Chapter 3

Dickens and the city: 'Animate London … inanimate London'

What is Dickens trying to describe? More often than not, it is London. He boasted in 1866 to know the city 'better than any one other man of all its millions'.[1] Certainly he began his complex relationship with the place early. John Forster started his biography with an account of how as a child being

> taken out for a walk into the real town, especially if it were anywhere about Covent-garden or the Strand, perfectly entranced him with pleasure. But, most of all, he had a profound attraction of repulsion to St. Giles's. If he could only induce whomsoever took him out to take him through Seven-dials, he was supremely happy. "Good Heaven!" he would exclaim, "what wild visions of prodigies of wickedness, want, and beggary, arose in my mind out of that place!" (*Forster* 11)

For many readers today, Dickens *is* nineteenth-century London and vice versa. Television and film directors spend immense amounts of money recreating authentic scenes of dilapidation and mud on the supposition that his fiction provides a window onto the nineteenth century and, above all, the street life of the city. The name 'Charles Dickens', of course, is part and parcel of the heritage London still sells to tourists today. A series of guidebooks even exists – *Walks in Dickens's London* – devoted to particular parts of the city and their relationship to the novels and the life of their author (a distinction not always very clearly maintained).[2]

If narrative point of view in Dickens is dynamic and often unstable, then it's scarcely surprising given how rapidly London was changing in the nineteenth century. Both the population and the built environment were subject to the transformation. Just under a million people lived in a built-up area of around five miles across at the beginning of the nineteenth century. By its end, the population of an area now seventeen miles across was over 6.5 million. The 1820s and 1830s, just when Dickens was beginning his career as a writer, were the years when the built environment of London was starting to undergo striking redevelopment under the aegis of the Prince Regent, later George IV. Dickens was in favour of London trying to match the splendours of nineteenth-century

Paris, celebrated as the visionary city at the end of *A Tale of Two Cities*, but he remained critical of what improvements were made and their frequent failure to make proper provision for the poor. The partial exception was the Victoria Embankment, which he admired. So rapid were the changes that went on during his career that in 1891 Justin McCarthy suggested there would soon need to be 'an edition of Dickens with copious explanatory notes on every page, or the younger readers will not know half the time what the author is talking about.'[3] Nothing was as spectacular a force for change as the railways, which boomed in the 1840s but remained an influence on the physical appearance of London for the rest of the century. When Dickens first came to London it was a place of horses and carts, the stagecoach was the harbinger of speed. The first of the London railways opened at the end of 1836, just as he was starting his career as a writer. Victoria Station opened in 1860. The world's first underground railway opened between Paddington and Farringdon Street in 1863. The railroad's transformation of the cityscape is described in *Dombey and Son* as a demonic force bringing chaos to what were then outer suburbs in Camden Town (where the Dickens family had lived in the 1820s):

> Everywhere were bridges that led nowhere; thoroughfares that were wholly impassable; Babel towers of chimneys, wanting half their height; temporary wooden houses and enclosures, in the most unlikely situations; carcases of ragged tenements, and fragments of unfinished walls and arches, and piles of scaffolding, and wildernesses of bricks, and giant forms of cranes, and tripods straddling above nothing. There were a hundred thousand shapes and substances of incompleteness, wildly mingled out of their places, upside down, burrowing in the earth, aspiring in the air, mouldering in the water, and unintelligible as any dream. Hot springs and fiery eruptions, the usual attendants upon earthquakes, lent their contributions of confusion to the scene. Boiling water hissed and heaved within dilapidated walls; whence, also, the glare and roar of flames came issuing forth; and mounds of ashes blocked up rights of way, and wholly changed the law and custom of the neighbourhood.   (*DS* 6, 79)

London here is Pandemonium, but Dickens was by no means constitutionally attached to 'law and custom', even if the passage describes the wreckage of a place he had lived in the 1820s. He could see in the chaos the railway brought, not least in its energy, a potential force for progress. When the railway reappears in the novel some chapters later, it seems to have transformed the area for the better, creating numerous opportunities, not least bringing relative prosperity to the amiable Toodle, who has become an engine fireman:

> Night and day the conquering engines rumbled at their distant work, or, advancing smoothly to their journey's end, and gliding like tame dragons into the allotted corners grooved out to the inch for their reception, stood bubbling and trembling there, making the walls quake, as if they were dilating with the secret knowledge of great powers yet unsuspected in them, and strong purposes not yet achieved. (*DS* 15, 245–6)

The ambivalence of Dickens's attitude to the railway is apparent in its final appearance in the novel as a demonic force, its 'red eyes bleared and dim', but one that scourges the villainous Carker from the narrative, 'whirled away upon a jagged mill, that spun him round and round, and struck him limb from limb, and licked his stream of life up with its fiery heat, and cast his mutilated fragments in the air' (*DS* 55, 842). This kind of cleansing violence occurs in many forms in Dickens. Here it doesn't assign any special moral role to the engine of the new industrial society, attacked so forcefully in *Hard Times*, but it does emphasize, at this stage at least, that he saw the new urban world as the source of a transformative power that could still be a force for good or ill. By the time he comes to write *Our Mutual Friend*, the potential for good seems to have dissipated, its energy degenerating into the entropy that seems to be wearing things out, as the railways tower threateningly 'still bestride the market-gardens that will soon die under them' (*OMF* 2: 1, 219).

'Energy' certainly remains an important word for Dickens across a range of contexts, but it is especially associated with the city Pip enters to find 'so crowded with people and so brilliantly lighted' (*GE* 2: 3, 185). Such arrival scenes are a feature of his writing from *Oliver Twist* onwards. Typically they are experienced as a bombardment of the senses. When in *Nicholas Nickleby* the hero and Smike arrive in the city, they find themselves dazzled 'by the quickly-changing and ever-varying objects' (*NN* 32, 390). The city is a market for a world of goods that 'jumbled each with the other, and flocking side by side, seemed to flit by in motley dance' (*NN* 32, 390–1). *Dombey and Son* shows Dickens was alert to the way the acceleration of modern life associated with the railways could change the experience of seeing the world:

> There are jagged walls and falling houses close at hand, and through the battered roofs and broken windows, wretched rooms are seen, where want and fever hide themselves in many wretched shapes, while smoke, and crowded gables, and distorted chimneys, and deformity of brick and mortar penning up deformity of mind and body, choke the murky distance. As Mr Dombey looks out of his carriage window, it is never in his thoughts that the monster who has brought him there has let the light of day in on these things: not made or caused them. (*DS* 20, 312)

Decades of experience looking out from railway carriages had by the end of the century 'prepared people to be film spectators'.[4] Although the train rushes onwards, the spectator of film remains still like the railway passenger, hit by a welter of impressions as the world flashes past.

Dickens's writing might even be regarded as an anticipation of cinema in its hunger to reproduce such impressions.[5] Various forms of public entertainment had been contributing towards the development of cinema through the nineteenth century, including the magic lantern, the panorama, and the diorama. These and other similar innovations often appear as tropes in Dickens's writing. Dickens described Paris as 'a moving panorama' (*L* 7: 724). In his travel book *Pictures of Italy* (1846), he wrote of the way the crowds of images he had gathered on his journey would stop, allow him to gaze at one of them steadily, and then 'dissolve, like a view in a magic-lantern' (*PI* 77). In 1857, he wrote to the actor William Macready about the public's hunger for 'more amusement, and particularly (as it strikes me) *something in motion*' (*L* 8: 399). Often it has proven difficult – as we saw in Chapter 2 – to discuss Dickens's mobile point of view without using the vocabulary of cinema editing. Sergei Eisenstein noticed one dissolve at the end of *A Tale of Two Cities*: 'Six tumbrils roll along the streets. Change these back again to what they were, thou powerful enchanter, Time, and they shall be seen to be the carriages of absolute monarchs, the equipages of feudal nobles, the toilettes of flaring Jezebels' (*TTC* 3: 15, 385).[6] In fact, even while Dickens was writing, contemporaries found it impossible not to compare his imagination to the visual technologies newly available to them: the camera lucida, the sun-picture, the photograph, and the daguerreotype were all invoked as comparisons by critics.[7]

Sometimes these commentators found him too open to the bombardment of the senses Victorians associated with the experience of modernity. Critics of sensational fiction in the 1860s often equated serial publication with a willingness to pander to urban restlessness. Margaret Oliphant complained, for instance, of 'the violent stimulant of serial publication … with its necessity for frequent and rapid recurrence of picquant situation'.[8] Dickens had chosen to pursue this kind of 'low' publication long before Oliphant made this judgement on his friend Collins's *The Woman in White*, but he also chose to stick at it. Rather than thinking in terms of a book that could be picked up and put aside in a leisurely manner, creating a bubble for escape, publishing in weekly or monthly parts meant that reading became part of the ebb and flow of daily life.[9] The pattern was effectively determined by a work-time discipline external to the reader. Completion of one installment meant deferring gratification until another was delivered. Serialization, from this point of view, represents another of those painful pleasures of modern life that Dickens explored so often: the awareness of seemingly unlimited potential allied to a frustrating limitation of access. The result according to critics was an experience of reading little better than 'distraction' (GE 2: 19, 300), the name Pip gives to his state of mind when he has to accompany Estella through the social whirl of London. The word implies a feverish and unsettled energy rather than the pleasures of contemplation. The German critic Walter Benjamin used it to describe the new urban consciousness derived from the city's welter of sensory impressions.[10]

Intrinsic to this escalation in the visual experience of nineteenth-century Londoners were advertisements. *Punch* complained the streets were blocked with vans exhibiting six-feet-high letters in 'bold black letter assertion'.[11] In 1855, the *Quarterly Review* described advertisements as 'the very daguerreotypes cast by the age which they exhibit, not done for effect, but faithful reflections of these insignificant items of life and things'.[12] Like Dickens's own prose, they insisted on the crowds in the street giving their attention – as Nicholas and Smike are forced to give their attention – to the 'tempting stores of everything to stimulate and pamper the sated appetite and give new relish to the oft-repeated feast' (*NN* 32, 390). Even if his novels often go back, as Dickens puts it at the opening of *Great Expectations*, to a time 'long before the days of photographs' (*GE* 1: 1, 3), the very acknowledgement of the new forms of technology and their increasing role in the lives of his readers only signals an awareness that he was fighting for space in the midst of bustling and aggressive visual culture. When visiting New York in 1867, such was the razzmatazz surrounding the visit that he wrote home to complain, 'I can't get down Broadway for my own portrait' (*L* 11: 527).

There was an intensifying demand in London to show the rapidly changing city to itself and to the world. Lord Byron's friend Lady Blessington recognized the market early on when she published *The Magic Lantern; or, Sketches of Scenes in the Metropolis* (1822). At its launch in 1842, *The Illustrated London News* promised 'to keep continually before the eye of the world a living and moving panorama of all its actions and influences'.[13] The illustrations with which Dickens published all his novels were an important part of their success (see Chapter 5), but they were also caught up in the visuality of Victorian commercial culture in other ways. The green covers of the monthly parts were prominent in Victorian bookstalls and usually provided a visual summary of the contents, at least of the variety of characters to be found there (see Figure 3.1). Inside, placed before the illustrations and then the text, were advertising supplements with their own pagination, 'The Pickwick Advertiser,' and so on. These were often intermeshed in various ways with the literary content of each part, adding to the distractions of the serial format. One innovative company, the Dakin Tea and Coffee Company, even copied the front-cover design into a full-page ad for its products, incorporated into the sixth monthly number of *Bleak House* (Figure 3.2).[14] Number 10 of *Martin Chuzzlewit*, issued in October 1843, came with a thirty-two-page pink-covered pamphlet bound to the back cover. At first glance, *The Pride of London: A Poem* looks like one of the many narcissistic literary accounts of the metropolis, but it turns out to be 'A description of the external & internal wonders of the Double Emporium of E. Moses & Son', tailors of Aldgate and the Minories. Following engravings of the two shops, it shifts into a verbal description of 'premises which long have been / The boast of London's busy scene.' In this same number, the novel itself introduces the reader to Mr Mould the undertaker's premises in Cheapside. Mould's shop manages to remain 'hard of hearing to the boisterous noises in the great main streets, and nestled in a quiet corner, where the city strife became a drowsy hum' (*MC* 25, 384). The same cannot be said of *Martin Chuzzlewit* as a whole, nor of any of the other novels. The advertising supplements contained plenty of ads for new editions of Dickens's other novels, and their many spin-offs. So, for instance, a reader of the first number of *Martin Chuzzlewit* in January 1843 would have encountered an ad from Mr Mitchell, bookseller, for an 'IMPORTANT ILLUSTRATION OF BOZ', that is, an engraving of Dolly Varden, whose vivacious presence in *Barnaby Rudge* had already sparked a fashion in bonnets.

Walking the streets of the great nineteenth-century cities, as Dickens frequently did in London, New York, and Paris, was to be subject to a constant visual bombardment in the newly gas-lit streets: unknown faces passing in the crowd, shop windows, advertisements posted everywhere. The German sociologist Georg Simmel studied the phenomenon of mental life in the new metropolitan cities of Europe. He gave a crisp statement of his idea of everyday life in nineteenth-century Paris: 'Interpersonal relations in big cities are distinguished by a marked preponderance of the activity of the eye over the activity of the ear.'[15] The same perception is implicit in the description of his methods Dickens gave in *Oliver Twist*, where he assumes his readers are the 'busy actors' of urban life, subject to the 'violent transitions and abrupt impulses of passion or feeling, which, presented before the eyes of mere spectators, are at once condemned as outrageous and preposterous' (*OT* 1: 17, 135). The visuality of Dickens's imagination was often commented upon, as we've seen already. His friend, the actor Macready, credited him with a 'clutching eye'. Others among his contemporaries described him as possessing 'a power of observation so enormous that he could photograph almost everything he saw.'[16] Dickens often positioned himself as 'an observant spectator', as he did in his preface to *A Tale of Two Cities* (*TTC* 397). Does any writer use 'eye' as a verb as often as Dickens? In *Oliver Twist*, Bumble 'eyed the building' where he meets Monks, 'with very

Figure 3.1 Wrapper for *Little Dorrit*, no. 7, June 1856. By permission of the Bodleian Library (ARCH AA d. 155).

Figure 3.2 'Dakin's Tea and Coffee Company', *Bleak House*, no. 6, August 1852. By permission of the Bodleian Library (ARCH AA. d. 40).

rueful looks' (*OT* 3: 1, 308). Taken up by Fagin, Noah Claypole is 'eyeing his new friend … with mingled fear and suspicion' (*OT* 3: 1, 355). The prevalence of the word in such relatively insignificant moments builds up incrementally the strong sense of characters looking and being looked *at* rather than simply being described *as* objects by detached observation from a stable point of view. Focalization can change rapidly within a single chapter or even passage, creating a kind of dizziness in the reader, what Eisenstein called 'the head-spinning tempo of changing impressions', creating distraction in the reader as he or she strives to work out what is really happening.[17]

A good example from a single passage comes in the description of Fagin entering the Three Cripples in *Oliver Twist*, a passage worth quoting at length to give the sense of rapidly changing points of view:

> It was curious to observe some faces which stood out prominently from among the group. There was the chairman himself, the landlord of the house: a coarse, rough, heavy-built fellow, who, while the songs were proceeding, rolled his eyes hither and thither, and, seeming to give himself up to joviality, had an eye for everything that was done, and an ear for everything that was said, – and sharp ones, too. Near him were the singers, receiving with professional indifference the compliments of the company, and applying themselves in turn to a dozen proffered glasses of spirits and water tendered by their more boisterous admirers, whose countenances, expressive of almost every vice in almost every grade, irresistibly attracted the attention by their very repulsiveness. Cunning, ferocity, and drunkenness in all its stages were there in their strongest aspects; and women – some with the last lingering tinge of their early freshness almost fading as you looked, and others with every mark and stamp of their sex utterly beaten out, and presenting but one loathsome blank of profligacy and crime; some mere girls, others but young women, and none past the prime of life, – formed the darkest and saddest portion of this dreary picture.
>
> Fagin, troubled by no grave emotions, looked eagerly from face to face while these proceedings were in progress, but apparently without meeting that of which he was in search. Succeeding, at length in catching the eye of the man who occupied the chair, he beckoned to him slightly, and left the room as quietly as he had entered it.   (*OT* 2: 4, 207)

The vocabulary of looking is omnipresent in the scene, making everything seem a question of someone's perspective. When Fagin steps into the room the reader seems to have his point of view, although, as in a carnival mirror, some things loom larger than others. As the list of these sights begins, the point of view switches to the landlord, who has an eye and ear for everything going on in the scene. He shifts from being the object of Fagin's look to become a viewing subject in his own right. Is it his 'attention' that is caught by the singers and their admirers, or Fagin's, or is the camera pulling back to give us a more detached view? Hardly the last perhaps, when the 'you' gets the reader involved in the scene, so close to the 'dreary picture', rather than allowing the distance of a detached observer. The final short paragraph brings the point of view back to Fagin as he moves from face to face and then meets the eye of the landlord from which the scene, a sentence or so before, had seemed to be viewed. The sense of a welter of sense impressions and crossfire of glances from different points of view is heightened in David Lean's film adaptation of this scene (see Figure 5.3) by conflating it with other scenes from the novel with Sikes and Nancy in them. In the film, her suspicious tracking of Fagin's interactions with the landlord, while pretending only to have eyes for Bill, reinforce the sense of the rapid crossfire of glances. Of course, it is Nancy's eyes – 'those widely-staring eyes' (*OT* 3: 10, 403) – that finally force Sikes to his death in the novel, a theme given a typical Dickensian comic counterpoint in Mr Bumble's misguided confidence in the power of his eyes to control Mrs Corney (*OT* 2: 14, 295–6).[18]

Looking from face to face without meeting an answering look, as Fagin does in the Three Cripples before meeting the eyes of the landlord, was taken by many to be a defining feature of the new urban experience of the nineteenth century. Benjamin, influenced by Simmel, gave a powerful account of the development of this new urban consciousness. He also developed the idea of the *flâneur* to describe the type of artist, like the poet Charles Baudelaire, who emerged from these new social conditions, drawn to the crowd, defensively self-concealed himself, but still able to create a new kind of art out of the 'daily shocks'.[19] Benjamin invoked a passage from Bulwer Lytton's novel *Eugene Aram* to describe the type of writing the *flâneur* might produce, with its glimpses of the self-enclosed world to be found in each passing individual in the crowd:

> What a world of dark and troublous secrets in the breast of every one
> who hurries by you! … what a gloomy and profound sublimity in
> the idea! – what a new insight it gives into the hearts of the common
> herd! – with what a strange interest it may inspire us for the humblest,
> the tritest passenger that shoulders us in the great thoroughfare of life!
> One of the greatest pleasures in the world is to walk alone, and at night,
> (while they are yet crowded,) through the long lamplit streets of this
> huge metropolis.[20]

The same idea of the crowd made of millions of self-enclosed worlds is found in the character of Nadgett in *Martin Chuzzlewit*:

> He was that sort of man that if he had died worth a million of money, or
> had died worth twopence halfpenny, everybody would have been per-
> fectly satisfied, and would have said it was just as they expected. And yet he
> belonged to a class; a race peculiar to the city; who are secrets as profound
> to one another, as they are to the rest of mankind.   (*MC* 27, 46)

Eugene Aram is a character accustomed to the sharp observance of a sea of strangers such as Nadgett. As many critics have pointed out, including Benjamin himself, Dickens often relishes the pleasures of losing himself in such a crowd and delving into its secret hearts.[21]

In *A Tale of Two Cities*, the narrator confesses his perverse indulgence in the experience of walking through the city at night:

> A wonderful fact to reflect upon, that every human creature is constituted to be that profound secret and mystery to every other. A solemn consideration, when I enter a great city by night, that every one of those darkly clustered houses encloses its own secret; that every room in every one of them encloses its own secret; that every beating heart in the hundreds of thousands of breasts there, is, in some of its imaginings, a secret to the heart nearest it! Something of the awfulness, even of Death itself, is referable to this.   (*TTC* 1: 3, 14–15)

Whereas human beings seem to live lives of quiet desperation, alienated and self-enclosed, the city itself often comes to vibrant life in the novels. Where Nadgett is a thing of mystery, in circulation around the city like a commodity, but seemingly unable to enter any kind of human communication, the city itself seems to live and breathe, the buildings gain a strange power of speech, more animated than the ghostly human presences that throng the streets:

> Thus, the revolving chimney-pots on one great stack of buildings, seemed to be turning gravely to each other every now and then, and whispering the result of their separate observation of what was going on below. Others, of a crook-backed shape, appeared to be maliciously holding themselves askew, that they might shut the prospect out and baffle Todgers's. The man who was mending a pen at an upper window over the way, became of paramount importance in the scene, and made a blank in it, ridiculously disproportionate in its extent, when he retired. The gambols of a piece of cloth upon the dyer's pole had far more interest for the moment than all the changing motion of the crowd. Yet even while the looker-on felt angry with himself for this, and wondered how it was, the tumult swelled into a roar; the host of objects seemed to thicken and expand a hundredfold; and after gazing, round him, quite scared, he turned into Todgers's again, much more rapidly than he came out; and ten to one he told M. Todgers afterwards that if he hadn't done so, he would certainly have come into the street by the shortest cut: that is to say, head-foremost.   (*MC* 9, 134)

In the early novels, such as *Martin Chuzzlewit*, the city has not quite become the machine for grinding human souls that it is in *Bleak House* and *Our Mutual Friend*, but even here this 'London … which hemmed Todgers's round and hustled it, and crushed it, and stuck its brick-and-mortar elbows into it, and kept the air from it, and stood perpetually between it and the light' (*MC* 9, 131) is overwhelming Martin as he tries to make his way through it, giving an intimation of the darker vision sustained in the later novels.

Dickens originally made a name for himself as the chronicler of this new life in the journalism he collected together in his first book, *Sketches by Boz* (1836). 'What inexhaustible food for speculation do the streets of London afford!' (*J* 1: 61) he insists at the opening of 'Shops and Their Tenants'. The sketches he collected in 'Scenes' – beginning with 'The Streets – Morning' and 'The Streets – Night' are devoted to recording as many aspects as possible of the street life of the metropolis. The popularity of the collection shows he was meeting a demand – most obvious in the newspapers and magazines which first published many of the sketches – for London to narrate itself to its inhabitants as it changed. The tenth monthly part of *Master Humphrey's Clock*, issued in January 1841, for instance, contained an ad for Charles Knight's *London* (1841–4), also initially published in monthly parts. The same author-publisher brought out *Knight's Cyclopedia of London* ten years later. The demand for such books sprang from the sense that the city was transforming itself, new places and experiences coming into being, while others were passing away. The taste for seeing the city as a place of constantly emerging new wonders was exploited by the tailors E. Moses & Son in their *Picture of London* advertisement. Their pitch was that their shops were new wonders in a city of new wonders. In Dickens, even in the early sketches such as 'Shops and Their Tenants', there's also a countervailing sense of things disappearing. In fact, that sketch seems to offer a story of steady decline, but at the very end the narrator's expectations are surprised:

> When we paused in front of our old friend, and observed these signs of poverty, which are not to be mistaken, we thought as we turned away, that the house had attained its lowest pitch of degradation. We were wrong. When we last passed it, a 'dairy' was established in the area, and a party of melancholy-looking fowls were amusing themselves by running in at the front door, and out at the back one. (*J* 1: 64)

The surprise, as it turns out, only confirms the sketch's opening claim about the 'inexhaustibility' of the city.

There are more threatening episodes in sketches such as 'St. Giles', an area, as Forster recorded, that always drew Dickens towards it. The sketch records the degradation and misery of some of the most oppressed areas of London, many of which were being demolished and redeveloped without any provision for their inhabitants, slum clearance producing only more overcrowding, squalor, and exploitation. Although in sketches like

'Thoughts about People' there is a sense of the loneliness endured by those who walk among the crowd, like the clerk who after his day's work returns to his 'little back room at Islington' (*J* 1: 213), the voice adopted by Boz tends towards amused detachment. If these streets are presented as 'an unknown region to our wandering mind' (*J* 1: xvi), they seem open to exploration and even ordering by Dickens. John Forster certainly seems to have taken a kind of comfort from the revelation of its 'interior hidden life', now made by Dickens as 'familiar as its commonest outward forms' (*Forster* 123). Dickens insisted in his original preface (1836) to the collection that his aim had been 'to present little pictures of life and manners as they really are' (*J* 1: xxix). Contemporaries such as Forster, who considered 'the observation shown throughout … nothing short of wonderful' (*Forster* 76), celebrated them in terms of realism. For Forster, part of the novelty was the new attention – in literature anyway – being given to 'a sort of life between the middle class and the low, which, having few attractions for bookish observers, was quite unhacknied ground' (*Forster* 77). There is no doubt that this socially unstable world between classes, peopled by those aiming for respectability and those who were being buffeted by the economic realities of the market-place, was the primary focus of the *Sketches*, but whether it is right for us to concede to Forster 'the absolute reality of the things depicted' is perhaps another matter.

These, after all, claim to be 'sketches', the word implying an impressionistic response, the product of the sensory bombardment I've been discussing, rather than the fully worked up picture of an omniscient observer at a distance. The results are certainly lively, but whether they obtain or even attempt the life-likeness of verisimilitude is another matter. Many of the sketches are extremely theatrical, not only because some, such as 'Private Theatres', explore the shows of London, but also because of the way the 'scenes' are presented to the reader. The talking chimney pots of *Martin Chuzzlewit* are anticipated, for instance, in the clothes that seem to take on a life of their own in 'Meditations in Monmouth Street':

> We have gone on speculating in this way, until whole rows of coats have started from their pegs, and buttoned up, of their own accord, round the waists of imaginary wearers; lines of trousers have jumped down to meet them; waistcoats have almost burst with anxiety to put themselves on; and half an acre of shoes have suddenly found feet to fit them, and gone stumping down the street with a noise which has fairly awakened us from our pleasant reverie, and driven us slowly away, with a bewildered stare, an object of astonishment to the good people of Monmouth Street, and of no slight suspicion to the policemen at the opposite street corner.   (*J* 1: 78)

The built environment of the streets seems to have a life of its own. Streets 'dart' before the reader, for instance, in 'Seven Dials (J1:72). The varieties of city life represented in the sketches live in complex interaction with London itself. What is revealed is not simply comic. 'Meditations in Monmouth Street' has its own misery, 'the bare and miserable room, destitute of furniture, crowded with his wife and children, pale, hungry, and emaciated; the man cursing their lamentations, staggering to the tap room, from whence he had just returned' (*J* 1: 80), but Boz is confident in his ability to guide us through it and to direct its tragic-comedy as a new kind of urban theatre.

Part of the drama that ensured the popular success of early novels such as *Oliver Twist* was also this thrilling revelation of parts of London unknown to polite readers, such as Jacob's Island, 'the strangest, the most extraordinary', Dickens boasts, 'of the many localities that are hidden in London, wholly unknown, even by name, to the great mass of its inhabitants' (*OT* 3: 12, 416). To the very end of his career, in *Our Mutual Friend*, Dickens continues to act as the reader's guide to marginal parts of London, such as the 'tract of suburban Sahara' (*OMF* 1: 4, 42) between Holloway and Battle Bridge where Boffin's mounds are heaped. Perhaps following the lead of Henry Mayhew's articles on 'Labour and the poor' which appeared in *The Morning Chronicle* over 1849–50, the later journalism Dickens published in his journals *Household Words* (1850–9) and *All the Year Round* (1859–93) often purports to fulfil a forensic desire in their middle-class readership to penetrate the hidden parts of the city as intense as any twenty-first-century television series devoted to crime-scene investigation.[22] By mid-century there was increasing paranoia about what was happening in the myriad nooks and out-of-the-way places found in the increasingly sprawling city: the poor were rumoured even to be breeding pigs in the sewers.[23] In 'A Detective Police Party' (*HW*, 27 July and 10 August 1850) and 'On Duty with Inspector Field' (*HW*, 14 June 1851), Dickens shows confidence in the knowledge of the New Police, especially in the person of Inspector Field, who was almost certainly the model for Bucket in *Bleak House*:

> I should like to know where Inspector Field was born. In Ratcliffe Highway, I would have answered with confidence, but for his being equally at home wherever we go. *He* does not trouble his head as I do, about the river at night. *He* does not care for its creeping, black and silent, on our right there, rushing through sluice gates, lapping at piles and posts and iron rings, hiding strange things in its mud, running away with suicides and accidentally drowned bodies faster than a midnight funeral should, and acquiring such various experience between its cradle and its grave. It has no mystery for *him*. Is there not the Thames Police! (*J* 2: 367)

The confident assertion with which the passage ends does not entirely tame the strange sense of the Thames being alive, 'creeping', 'rushing', 'hiding', 'running away', its protean forms keep it always slightly ahead of the police. The end of the essay provides not disclosure, not the end of the mystery, but the sense of a process in abeyance, soon able to come to life again:

> As to White, who waits on Holborn Hill to show the courts that are eaten out of Rotten Gray's Inn Lane, where other lodging-houses are, and where (in one blind alley) the Thieves' Kitchen and Seminary for the teaching of the art to children, is, the night has so worn away, being now
>
> almost at odds with morning, which is which, that they are quiet, and no light shines through the chinks in the shutters. As undistinctive Death will come here, one day, sleep comes now. The wicked cease from troubling sometimes, even in this life.   (*J* 2: 369)

'Sometimes' is not a word to bring the reader in the sprawling city too much comfort.

Likewise, Inspector Bucket in *Bleak House* and the 'neat' and 'methodical' (*OMF* 1: 3, 33) Inspector in *Our Mutual Friend* are efficient enough, but they do not finally get to the heart of the matter. If Bucket manages to solve the murder, he fails to find Lady Dedlock in time. In *Our Mutual Friend*, only the accidental meeting between Mortimer Lightwood and John Rokesmith brings the mystery of John Harmon to light, and even that has to be explained to the Inspector by the murdered man. London is too much of an intricate puzzle for the forensic intelligence to resolve. In *All the Year Round*, Dickens developed the persona of 'The Uncommercial Traveller' for himself and created some of his most brilliant writing about the city. Far from seeking out the forensic truth, like the police, this persona drifts in and out of the city's alleys and lanes gathering impressions. In 'Night Walks', for instance, he describes how in 'the course of those nights, I finished my education in a fair amateur experience of houselessness' (*J* 4: 150). In 'On an Amateur Beat', the Uncommercial Traveller imagines a later generation of geological enquirers discovering the fossilized footprints of the street scene around him: 'I wonder whether the race of men then to be our successors on the earth could, from these or any marks, by the utmost force of the human intellect, unassisted by tradition, deduce such an astounding inference as the existence of a polished state of society that bore with the public savagery of neglected children in the streets of its capital city, and was proud of its power by sea and land, and never used its power to siege and save them!' (*J* 4: 382). The double-voiced mockery of the language of forensic deduction draws the contrast with his investigations, which are based on glimpses and sudden moments of illumination from within the larger mystery.

While composing *Dombey and Son* in 1846, Dickens had written to Forster from Lausanne to express the difficulties of writing with any speed without the stimulating presence of the city and its teeming streets:

> But the difficulty of going at what I call a rapid pace, is prodigious: it is almost an impossibility. I suppose this is partly the effect of two years' ease, and partly of the absence of streets and numbers of figures. I can't express how much I want these. It seems as if they supplied something to my brain, which it cannot bear, when busy, to lose. For a week or a fortnight I can write prodigiously in a retired place (as at Broadstairs), and a day in London sets me up again and starts me. But the toil and labour of writing, day after day, without that magic lantern, is IMMENSE!!   (*L* 4: 612)

London is the 'magic lantern', the great modern show (tending towards cinema) with light, action, and crowds. Without it, Dickens's productivity slackened. His letter implies he is an addict in need of stimulation. London for Dickens was a discomforting object of desire: the marketplace of the painful pleasures of modern life and the theatre of the 'attraction of repulsion'. Smithfield Market often seems to be the heart of London in this regard, usually appearing early on as a scene of arrival for his characters. When Oliver first enters London, it is a confusing experience, but when he encounters Smithfield confusion turns to riot and the complete overwhelming of the senses. Smithfield represents the city as a nightmarish slaughterhouse, ignoring suffering in the constant 'to and fro', concerned only with profit:

> Countrymen, butchers, drovers, hawkers, boys, thieves, idlers, and vagabonds of every low grade, were mingled together in a dense mass: the whistling of drovers, the barking of dogs, the bellowing and plunging of beasts, the bleating of sheep, and grunting and squeaking of pigs; the cries of hawkers, the shouts, oaths, and quarrelling on all sides, the ringing of bells and roar of voices that issued from every public-house; the crowding, pushing, driving, beating, whooping, and yelling; the hideous and discordant din that resounded from every corner of the market; and the unwashed, unshaven, squalid, and dirty figures constantly running to and fro, and bursting in and out of the throng, rendered it a stunning and bewildering scene which quite confounded the senses.   (*OT* 1: 21, 171)

The confounding of the senses produced by a weltering list of words is a familiar device in Dickens, especially in relation to the overwhelming power of the crowd, here with livestock and humans becoming almost interchangeable in their distress. In *Great Expectations*, Jaggers has his office close by, where he transacts its own ghastly trade in human futures. In case the

parallel be lost on his readers, Dickens has Pip visit the market while waiting
for his lawyer:

> When I told the clerk that I would take a turn in the air while I waited,
> he advised me to go round the corner and I should come into Smith-
> field. So, I came into Smithfield; and the shameful place, being all
> asmear with filth and fat and blood and foam, seemed to stick to me.
> So, I rubbed it off with all possible speed by turning into a street where
> I saw the great black dome of Saint Paul's bulging at me from behind
> a grim stone building which a bystander said was Newgate Prison.
> Following the wall of the jail, I found the roadway covered with straw
> to deaden the noise of passing vehicles; and from this, and from the
> quantity of people standing about, smelling strongly of spirits and beer,
> I inferred that the trials were on. (*GE* 2: 1, 165)

Pip feels he can never rub off the stain on his character, nor does he ever
entirely escape from the idea of the city as a huge prison, the trope that had
dominated *Little Dorrit*. The feeling of unease with a city full of teeming life,
but whose purposes often seem directed towards mangling or at least imprisoning and thwarting its human inhabitants, is one that only intensifies in the
later novels. If the city has a rough comic life in *Martin Chuzzlewit*, then in
the later fiction its animation provides a much more intimidating presence, as
when the houses in Little Britain, hard by the 'shameful place' of Smithfield,
seem to Pip to be 'looking as if they had twisted themselves to peep down
at me' (*GE* 2: 1,164). Later, in Gerrard Street, coming into 'a sudden glare of
gas', the city seems 'all alight and alive with that inexplicable feeling I had had
before' (*GE* 2: 14, 269). Now the city, even with its life and energy, has become
a great mystery.

The idea gets its most famous expression in the opening pages of *Bleak
House*, in one of the greatest passages Dickens ever wrote:

> LONDON. Michaelmas Term lately over, and the Lord Chancellor sit-
> ting in Lincoln's Inn Hall. Implacable November weather. As much mud
> in the streets, as if the waters had but newly retired from the face of the
> earth, and it would not be wonderful to meet a Megalosaurus, forty feet
> long or so, waddling like an elephantine lizard up Holborn Hill. Smoke
> lowering down from chimney-pots, making a soft black drizzle, with
> flakes of soot in it as big as full-grown snow-flakes – gone into mourn-
> ing, one might imagine, for the death of the sun. Dogs, undistinguish-
> able in mire. Horses, scarcely better; splashed to their very blinkers.
> Foot passengers, jostling one another's umbrellas, in a general infection
> of ill-temper, and losing their foot-hold at street-corners, where tens of
> thousands of other foot passengers have been slipping and sliding since

> the day broke (if the day ever broke), adding new deposits to the crust
> upon crust of mud, sticking at those points tenaciously to the pavement,
> and accumulating at compound interest.   (*BH* 1, 13)

This tour de force collects together much of the Dickensian response to London. From *Sketches by Boz*, there is the sense of the city as a multi-layered history, but now it seems to stretch back to prehistoric times, and to be ruptured
rather than merely stratified by its past. Dinosaurs loom up from the past in
an uncanny fashion, the recognizable outlines of what ought not to be there.
Fog makes all outlines indistinct, mud blurs the distinction between water and
earth:

> Fog everywhere. Fog up the river, where it flows among green aits and
> meadows; fog down the river, where it rolls defiled among the tiers of
> shipping and the waterside pollutions of a great (and dirty) city. Fog on
> the Essex marshes, fog on the Kentish heights. Fog creeping into the
> cabooses of collier-brigs; fog lying out on the yards, and hovering in
> the rigging of great ships; fog drooping on the gunwales of barges and
> small boats. Fog in the eyes and throats of ancient Greenwich pension-
> ers, wheezing by the firesides of their wards; fog in the stem and bowl
> of the afternoon pipe of the wrathful skipper, down in his close cabin;
> fog cruelly pinching the toes and fingers of his shivering little 'prentice
> boy on deck. Chance people on the bridges peeping over the parapets
> into a nether sky of fog, with fog all round them, as if they were up in a
> balloon, and hanging in the misty clouds.
>   Gas looming through the fog in divers places in the streets, much as
> the sun may, from the spongey fields, be seen to loom by husbandman
> and ploughboy. Most of the shops lighted two hours before their time –
> as the gas seems to know, for it has a haggard and unwilling look.
>
> (*BH* 1, 13–14)

The courts, where truth and justice ought to be discerned, seem mired in it.
Like a film director jump-cutting between shots, the reiterated word 'fog' pre-
cipitates us across different locations without giving any sense of the relation
between them, apart from the fact they are all linked by being only dimly available to view. They are all somewhere in London, but how are they related to
each other? Grotesque the passage certainly is, but not in the familiar sense of
giving inanimate objects a human form; it is too foggy to make out properly
even such a transformation. The only thing available to personification seems
to be the 'gas', struggling to be seen through the haze, 'haggard and unwilling'.
    Not much enlightenment here then in the great world city. Despite the vigi-
lance and persistence of Inspector Bucket, who initially, anyway, seems to be
allied with the withering hand of Tulkinghorn, hounding Gridley and Jo to

their deaths, things come to light only fleetingly and unexpectedly in *Bleak House*. The city is as obscure and hard to read as any document in it. Clarity seems like a distant memory, perhaps only a fairy tale, like the brook 'clear as crystal', Snagsby tells his apprentices, which 'once ran right down the middle of Holborn, when Turnstile really was a turnstile, leading slap away into the meadows' (*BH* 10, 158). Snagsby himself has never seen the brook, only heard tell of it. This London exists like a legend or a visionary city beneath the urban sprawl that built up over Dickens's lifetime. By *Little Dorrit*, still 'gloomy, close, and stale' (*LD* 1: 3, 43), London is not simply an obscure text or document but a huge prison, trapping its population, whether they are inside or outside the Marshalsea. It doesn't just evade attempts to make sense of it but imprisons those who would try. Returning from his years abroad, Arthur Clennam finds his mother confined to her house, prisoner to some past misdeed he struggles to comprehend through the novel. Later she describes herself 'in prison, and in bonds here' (*LD* 1: 5, 64). Taken to Fredrick Dorrit's rooms in Lant Street, Arthur finds them like a cell, 'a sickly room, with a turn-up bedstead in it' (*LD* 1: 9, 107). Mrs Chivery's shop, despite its attempts at respectability, is in the shadow of another famous London prison in Horsemonger's Lane. Mrs Gowan, says her son, lives in a 'dreary red-brick dungeon at Hampton Court' (*LD* 1: 27, 330). So prisons – literal and metaphorical – proliferate across London, but primarily people are imprisoned by themselves and by their pasts. *Little Dorrit* is peopled by self-tormentors, those who refuse to accept the possibility raised by the working title of the novel: 'Nobody's Fault'. What the trope of the prison may not have adequately expressed for Dickens was his sense of the city and its past as both imprisoning and productive, that sense of energy captured in the final phrase of the novel, when Arthur and Amy step down into its 'roaring streets'.

For Dickens, the city is more often a great engine, like the novels themselves, spitting out and swallowing characters, sometimes transforming them for the better but consigning many others to the dustbin of history. In this far-from-equitable process of winnowing, subjecting everything for better or worse to its rotating blades, the city approximates the grinding machines of *Hard Times* and *A Tale of Two Cities*. The city is the place where the law operates like a great mill. *Our Mutual Friend* has perhaps the fullest sense of the city as a combine harvester of souls; crowds are poured into it, some, like Eugene, to be freed from their husks, others like irredeemable waste spewing out at the other end. Perhaps not exactly 'out'. Like a prison, everyone seems trapped, but now in circulation in a convoluted and leaking system. Bodies are forced through its by-ways just as Eugene Wrayburn drags Bradley Headstone around the various 'No Thoroughfares' at the dead of night. None of the other novels crosses the city quite so extensively. After the opening chapter on the river, an emblem of the city itself, the action switches to a journey from west to east across the city. From the dinner party of the Veneerings held in the West End, Eugene and Mortimer pass the Monument, the Tower of London, and St Katherine's Docks. From Rotherhithe, 'where accumulated scum of humanity seemed to be washed from higher grounds, like so much moral sewage' (*OMF* 1: 3, 30), they press on even further into the East End, going down the social scale as they go across the city, before arriving in Limehouse to confront more flotsam and jetsam, in the form of the body identified as John Harmon's. Harmon's body, we later discover, has been shot out into the river, like the human excrement emptied untreated out of the sewers that produced the century's cholera epidemics. Harmon has been drugged and nearly murdered, his identity almost dissolved, 'But it was not I. There was no such thing as I, within my knowledge' (*OMF* 2: 13, 363). From this dissolution, he is returned to life, but his resurrection depends on the death of John Harmon, for a time at least, as he re-enters the plot first as Julius Handford and then as John Rokesmith. 'Come up and be dead!' (*OMF* 2: 6, 280), cries Jenny Wren to Fascination Fledgeby, who, grinding his financial mill, cannot understand her words. John Harmon has already understood the idea of a death that is more than life. Cast up out of the Thames, he resolves to be dead in order to discover what life there is for him in the city. Jenny's exhortation implies that death on the rooftops is more like living than life on the grinding streets below. Others seem trapped in a mill of living death, like Bradley Headstone, ground through the streets by Eugene, but also trapped in a system of respectability that only exacerbates the volcanic 'nature' he is forced to keep down. Bodies enter the river, some are drowned, others return to life, only to drown a second time, such as Riderhood, and still others survive, such as John Harmon. Not even the dead, if the dust heaps and the body parts that stock Mr Venus's shop are anything to go by, ever really escape the great grinding wheels of the city. Everything must go around again it seems.

At the end of the novel, Mortimer Lightwood stumbles on the word 'society'. He revisits the West End to see what High Society has to make of the story of Eugene and Lizzie. Through Twemlow's unexpected defiance, Dickens seems to be insisting on a meritocratic definition of social roles in the modern city, but what is left unanswered by the end of the novel is the stumbling block of society. How do things fit together? Earlier, Wegg had complimented Venus on his ability to 'fit together on wires the whole framework of society' (*OMF* 3: 6, 472). If the resolutions of the plot reward Mr Venus the articulator with animation of the heart, he seems to have gained it at the cost of any pretension to understand the broader relations of what might be called 'society'. Ending with the figures of Mortimer and Twemlow, who succeed in their rebellion against the tyranny of Lady Tippins and Podsnap, the question is left open as to how they relate to anyone else. Even the small group that clusters around the Boffins, including Eugene and Lizzie, appears to be an idyll whose place within the larger labyrinth elaborated by the novel remains uncertain.

Chapter 4

Dickens, gender, and domesticity: 'Be it ever … so ghastly … there's no place like it'

The idyllic group of those who survive in *Our Mutual Friend* is very much conceived of as a domestic circle. Bella's right to her position as the wife of John Rokesmith and then, more properly, John Harmon, is signalled in her command of the *Complete British Family Housewife* (*OMF* 4: 5, 666). The snug group of the family seems to offer the only shelter from the external world and its forces in most of the novels Dickens wrote. Those pressures are most often constituted in terms of the grinding alienation and degradation of London, the Victorian world city. In *Barnaby Rudge* and then *A Tale of Two Cities*, the only two historical novels he wrote, the domestic circle seems the best refuge against the impersonal forces of change in history. Dickens had an important role in creating the idea of the sanctity of the family for the nineteenth century and beyond, not least in the domestic gathering at Christmas. In the novels, however, the family is scarcely ever a stable institution, especially at the outset of the plots, but even those groups who survive and prosper are not usually naturalized into happy clusters. Bella, after all, turns out to have married and made herself happy with the 'wrong' man, who turns out to be the 'right' man for whom she was originally intended as part of his inheritance, 'willed away', as she puts it, 'like a horse, or a dog, or a bird' (*OMF* 2: 13, 371). The Boffins, who act as the couple's guardian angels, have had to supply all the affection her husband has ever known in default of his cruel father. Old John Harmon had effectively dispossessed both his children and set in play the train of events that John and the Boffins put right through their pious fraud on Bella. Even then, the question of the relationship between this group and the larger structure of society is a complex one. Neither at the beginning nor the end of the novel do family groups seem the building blocks assumed by any normative idea of domestic ideology: the version of the family unity (with the father at the head and the mother tending to the children at home) as a kind of organic cell endlessly reproduced in the larger body of society never quite works out in Dickens.

An exhaustive survey of the inhabitants of the Dickens world reveals that only fifteen significant characters from the major works had or have two parents, 'and in nearly half of these cases their families today would be considered dysfunctional'.[1] The number of orphans among the major characters in the novels emphasizes the struggle involved in creating the family circles that come together in their closing pages. Those who survive the tribulations of history and society have often had to create for themselves communities not straightforwardly familial, like John Harmon and the Boffins, asserting 'the claims of the nat'ral affections' (*OMF* 1: 7, 95) against the failure of blood relations to act according to their proper 'nature'. Similarly, if the domestic circle is often centred on the dutiful 'little' woman in the house, as it frequently is in the novels, then this woman often has to undertake an arduous journey beyond the house, like Nell in *The Old Curiosity Shop* or Florence cast out 'in the streets' in *Dombey and Son* (47, 721), in order to restore its fortunes. In the process, these women take the risk of either succumbing to or even themselves turning into versions of those marginalized females who are sometimes left as an uneasy presence disturbing whatever resolution is achieved at the end of the novels.

Few commentators can resist linking these complications to the difficulties of family life experienced by Dickens himself. His childhood was blighted by his father's impecunious nature, and he never felt properly loved by his parents. The recurrent figure of the orphan or the neglected child, especially in *David Copperfield*, no doubt speaks to this feeling. Nor, later, was his marriage a happy one. From at least the early 1850s, he spoke of a lack of warmth between himself and Catherine Hogarth Dickens, whom he had married in 1836. His sister-in-law, Georgina Hogarth, seems to have taken on the duties of housekeeper and hostess after the American tour of 1842. In 1857, the couple moved to separate bedrooms, the door between them being boarded up, and in 1858 they formally split, with all the children, except the eldest boy Charley, staying with their father. The situation was complicated by rumours of an affair between Dickens and Georgina, and then of his infatuation with the young actress, Ellen Ternan (1839–1914), which continued until his death. Dickens had met Ternan at Manchester in August 1857, when she acted in a production of *The Frozen Deep*, the play Dickens helped Wilkie Collins write. This situation must have been painful enough for all those involved, but on 7 June 1858 Dickens took the extraordinary step of publishing a personal statement in *The Times*, reprinted in *Household Words* on 12 June, denying rumours about the involvement of other women (*L* 8: 744). The grist supplied to the gossip's mill was then increased by the revelations of 'The Violated Letter' (*L* 8: 740–1), as Dickens called it, a private correspondence to his American manager, which somehow came into the hands of the press. The letter blamed the separation on Catherine's constitutional coldness, among other things, but there has always been a suspicion that Dickens may have had a hand in leaking the document. Unhappy homes, suspicious relationships with the hint of incest, boarded-up rooms, and letters going astray: Dickens's personal life has the air of a sensation novel.

Even so, there is no doubt that Dickens wished to make himself an important spokesman for the domestic virtues. The journal *Household Words*, as its title suggests, was designed to fulfil his ambitions in this regard. Many thought he had already gone a long way towards it in the novels, an attitude *Fraser's Magazine* confirmed in its December 1850 review of *David Copperfield*: 'There is not a fireside in the kingdom where the cunning fellow has not contrived to secure a corner for himself as one of the dearest, and, by this time, one of the oldest friends of the family' (*Collins a* 244). The Christmas Books, and especially the first, *A Christmas Carol*, published in 1843, played a huge part in defining the idea of Christmas as a small family circle gathered together around the hearth, putting aside the world of getting and spending in order to celebrate more fully human relations. When he gave public readings of *A Christmas Carol*, he encouraged his audience to think of themselves as 'a group of friends, listening to a tale told by a winter fire' (*Speeches* 246). This wished transmutation of paying customers into friends and family seems to indicate the importance of the idea of the domestic circle in the nineteenth century to papering over the alienated relations of the marketplace. 'Family' in this sense of a small group of blood relations sharing the same domestic space was by this time replacing more aristocratic ideas of dynasty, located in the great house rather than anything more homely, where blood was more important for the transmission of a name and title than as a locus for what middle-class thinking represented as the natural affections between parent and child.

Blood relationships remained important to the middle classes for the transmission of property and the idea of what family members owed each other as an intrinsic bond of nature, but these relationships were naturalized precisely in terms of the affections rather than the perpetuation of a family name. In *Barnaby Rudge*, Sir John Chester is the epitome of the nineteenth-century idea of the unfeeling aristocrat of the eighteenth century, concerned as he is with surface presentation and name, showing no affection for his son Edward, smirking at 'the filial affections, and all that sort of thing' (*BR* 32, 268) when encouraging him to make a marriage for money that will benefit them both financially. When Edward finally marries Emma Haredale, the niece of his father's hated rival, against his father's wishes, an old dynastic feud is ended. 'Let our ill-fated house remain the ruin it is' (*BR* 79, 659), says her uncle, consigning the great house of the aristocracy to the past. The reconciliation takes place in the middle-class home of the genial Gabriel Varden the locksmith.

Edward is effectively being redeemed for a new formation of family relations. In *Bleak House*, as one might expect from a much more sophisticated novel than *Barnaby Rudge*, Sir Leicester Dedlock is a more complicated case of the same historical determinism, capable of forgiving his wife when he discovers the truth of the past, but nonetheless rendered by Dickens a victim to the dynastic ideas of the aristocratic caste. Indeed, his wife's deeds fulfil the curse against the Dedlock family for its adherence to the Royalist cause in the Civil War. History itself seems to have written the demise of the aristocratic family in most of the novels. More mundanely, the rumbling inadequacies of the Court of Chancery appear as a sign of the failure of the old order to transmit its family values, a situation only righted at the end when John Jarndyce resigns his interest in Esther and, as it were, releases her from the name that has been milled through decades of Chancery.

The ideology of the middle-class family – not by any means what actually happened in practice in Victorian society at large – depended on a division of gender roles between the female space of the household and the public world of commerce (and history) into which husbands and sons went each day. Dickens seems to have subscribed to an idea of female nature as more naturally benevolent than men's. So powerful does it seem to be at times in the novels that it can break through the surface of years of corruption to assert itself, even against a woman's own self-interest, as when Nancy saves Oliver from Fagin's schemes or Sophronia Lammle saves Georgina from her own machinations. From the point of view of this domestic ideology, the home was frequently represented as a sanctified space, kept apart from the world of conflict and struggle outside, a place to which men could return for bodily and spiritual refreshment. The woman in it, if she performed properly, was thought of as an angelic being. Even if she was not encouraged to use her wings and fly very far, she was deemed able to bestow a kind of spiritual absolution on the husband returning from the taint of the world outside. Such is the power of Florence's 'strange ethereal light' in *Dombey and Son* (47, 707) or Agnes's 'face shining on me like a Heavenly light' at the end of *David Copperfield* (64, 805).

For Dickens, this power of domestic absolution often seems stronger in spiritual terms than the official institutions of the Church: the domestic becomes a kind of religion. The ideal was given an influential poetic statement in Coventry Patmore's *The Angel in the House* (1854–63), a series of poems on married love. In *Our Mutual Friend*, Bella studies to make herself the kind of housewife who can give succour on a daily basis to John when he comes home from the China House. Contrasted with these homely and interior virtues, the female aristocrat was likely to be thought of as a creature of surface, with no inner feelings, and an over-concern for appearances and social status. Lady Tippins – superficial sponsor of the significantly named Veneerings in *Our Mutual Friend* – is a satire on the aristocratic woman:

> Betimes next morning, that horrible old Lady Tippins (relict of the late Sir Thomas Tippins, knighted in mistake for somebody else by His Majesty King George the Third, who, while performing the ceremony, was graciously pleased to observe, 'What, what, what? Who, who, who? Why, why, why?') begins to be dyed and varnished for the interesting occasion. She has a reputation for giving smart accounts of things, and she must be at these people's early, my dear, to lose nothing of the fun. Whereabout in the bonnet and drapery announced by her name, any fragment of the real woman may be concealed, is perhaps known to her maid; but you could easily buy all you see of her, in Bond Street; or you might scalp her, and peel her, and scrape her, and make two Lady Tippinses out of her, and yet not penetrate to the genuine article.
>
> (*OMF* 1: 10, 122)

Tippins is defined as a 'relict' of a system that for Dickens is an anachronism. Even her title ought by right to belong to somebody else, and does not even date very far back, the incidental mockery of George III as a booby only confirming the scant regard shown in the novel for the whole system of titles and hereditary rights. When Pip gets seduced by gentility in *Great Expectations* (1: 19, 155), he starts to feel himself 'all face', becoming a façade like Lady Tippins, a woman of pure surface impossible to get beyond, for whom name and rank is everything, and merit and 'energy' of the kind Lizzie shows in saving Eugene nothing. In this regard, Lady Tippins is the comic repetition of the much more complex figure from *Bleak House*: Lady Dedlock, all icy surface, is a study of a woman who seems the epitome of aristocratic hauteur, haunted by the reality of her social origins and, more particularly, the stain brought on her history by the birth of an illegitimate daughter. In this regard, unlike Lady Tippins, her icy façade covers very turbulent waters indeed. The emotional heart of the novel is her relationship with her 'natural' child Esther, a relationship blighted and never fully allowed expression, at least in part because of the question of what it would do to the Dedlock name.

Compared to such grand women, defined by their surface veneer, Dickens offers a series of 'little' women, defined by their 'heart' and their care for the interiors of the home. These include Florence Dombey, Agnes Copperfield, Esther Summerson and 'Little' Amy Dorrit among them, but also minor characters such as Biddy in *Great Expectations* or Polly Toodle in *Dombey and Son* who the narrator takes to be 'a good plain sample of nature that is ever, in the mass, better, truer, higher, nobler, quicker to feel, and much more constant to retain, all tenderness and pity, self-denial and devotion, than the nature of men' (*DS* 3, 40). These and the other many little women maintain or come to maintain spaces that are homes rather than the great houses of the aristocracy. These angels are for the most part practical as well as ethereal, to be contrasted with those like Dora Spenlow, the 'child-bride' in *David Copperfield*, who lack the ability and energy to maintain a household. Dora's loss of heart and eventual death gives a sense of the importance of the practical household virtues to Dickens's meritocratic version of the Angel in the House. Grand houses in the novels, such as Chesney Wold, the ancestral home of the Dedlocks, are haunted by their pasts in ways that look back to the critique of aristocratic power found in the castles and dungeons of Gothic novels.[2] Although the grand spaces are not always strictly aristocratic in Dickens, they are usually linked to the death of domestic feeling and the sense of dark deeds from the past hanging over them. So the Dombey 'mansion' in its 'grim reality' gains a 'reputation ... as a haunted house' (*DS* 23, 355); so too, most strikingly, does Satis House in *Great Expectations*, built with the money of a brewing dynasty, remain haunted by Miss Havisham's past. Both of them have fallen victim to a disregard for what Dickens values as homely virtues. Such disregard is usually punished in the fiction, whatever the pathos finally given to the fates of those involved in the cases of Sir Leicester and Miss Havisham. Although Eugene Wrayburn is a scion of the upper classes who explicitly mocks the 'domestic virtues' (*OMF* 2: 6, 281–2), he proves to be open to redemption by the love (and 'energy') of Lizzie Hexham, one of the Dickens household angels. Eugene's lack of energy and disdain for the word itself (*OMF* 1: 3, 29) marks him as enervated by the withering touch of nobility (in the form of 'my respected father' – the 'M. R. F.' [1: 12, 149] as Eugene prefers to put it). Fitting out a kitchen in the private chambers he shares with Mortimer, Eugene mocks 'the moral influence of these objects, in forming the domestic virtues' (*OMF* 2: 6, 282). The flour-barrel, rolling pin, and kettle show that he continues to mistake the 'heart' Dickens associates with the hearth for the things that are merely gathered around it. His joking about the domestic virtues serves as a reminder from Dickens to the reader who might be won over by his easy wit that he is still caught between the role of aristocratic seducer and his later, more genuine understanding of Lizzie's virtues, an indication reinforced by the seriousness of Mortimer's response to his trifling. Reducing this aspect of the plot to an allegory, which Dickens never does, one could suggest he has to be scourged by Bradley Headstone, the self-made man whose own lowly origins he has cruelly mocked (*OMF* 2: 6, 285), before he can truly appreciate the values of Lizzie's virtues. If the novel refuses to play itself out in such rigorously allegorical terms, it is partly because the tortures undergone by Bradley at the hands of Eugene's 'chafing' and then Riderhood's more malignant designs threaten to become the dramatic focus of the closing chapters. In their intensity, these scenes almost overwhelm the series of neat closures in the other plot lines, but Bradley's violence speaks to a submerged element of class vengeance at work in the construction of the plot. Like the sympathies Dickens showed for the Gordon Rioters in *Barnaby Rudge*, to the alarm of some of his friends, the violence of Headstone's attack on Wrayburn is at least partially the expression of a revolutionary side to his antipathy to the old aristocratic order. The violence often visited upon the houses of the great in the novels suggests an anger bubbling beneath the surface well beyond any straightforward affirmation of middle-class family values.

Dickens often suggests that without the distortions of greed and selfishness human sympathies are naturally benevolent, especially for women, finding their best expression in family relations but potentially extending beyond them. The best souls, such as Esther Summerson, seem able to reach out and touch the hearts of everyone with whom they come into contact. What Dickens is equally clear about is the warping and perverting pressures exerted on human nature by a range of influences. He explores the question explicitly in a passage addressed to the reader in *Dombey and Son*:

> It might be worth while, sometimes, to inquire what Nature is, and how men work to change her, and whether, in the enforced distortions so produced, it is not natural to be unnatural. Coop any son or daughter of our mighty mother within narrow range, and bind the prisoner to one idea, and foster it by servile worship of it on the part of the few timid or designing people standing round, and what is Nature to the willing captive who has never risen up upon the wings of a free mind – drooping and useless soon – to see her in her comprehensive truth!   (*DS* 47, 700)

Under pressure from such influences, the human affections often present something of a tangled skein. Even when they seem to be operating on behalf of naturalized familial relations, they seem capable of being distorted into savage and destructive forces. In *Barnaby Rudge*, Edward Chester's virtuous desire to play the 'manly open part' (*BR* 15, 131) looks naive compared with his later recognition that there may be such things as 'monsters of affection' (*BR* 79, 664). In the same novel, Simon Tappertit, the apprentice boy whose 'soul' threatens to get 'into his head' with wild ideas, tells the repressed servant Mrs Miggs that 'there are strings … in the human heart that had better not be wibrated' (*BR* 22, 189). What these strings are and how they should be played upon is an enquiry each of the novels undertakes in its own way. In *Barnaby Rudge*, for instance, the fierce passions of the 'centaur' Hugh – half man and seemingly half savage beast – make him the natural leader of the mob that attempts to tear down the walls of Newgate, but it emerges his anger

is the product of his sympathy with his mother, hanged by the bloody code
of eighteenth-century law for a minor theft. The maternal bond in his case,
like the equally 'strange promptings of nature' (*BR* 68, 566) that unite Barnaby
and his father, are remorseless, moving, and, at the same time, dangerously
destructive. In the same novel, Dickens describes the crowd that tries to tear
down Newgate in terms that seem drawn from his friend Thomas Carlyle's
idea of the mob as an elemental force figured in terms of volcanic flows and
oceanic convulsions: 'Assembling and dispersing with equal suddenness, it is
as difficult to follow to its various sources as the sea itself; nor does the parallel
stop here, for the ocean is not more fickle and uncertain, more terrible when
roused, more unreasonable, or more cruel' (*BR* 52, 429). Nothing could seem
more different from the ties of natural sympathy and tenderness Dickens identifies with family feeling, until later he reveals the mob threatening Newgate
includes some members motivated by the promptings of precisely this nature:

> There was more than one woman there, disguised in man's attire, and
> bent upon the rescue of a child or brother. There were the two sons of
> a man who lay under sentence of death, and who was to be executed
> along with three others, on the next day but one.   (*BR* 63, 522)

A few pages later, describing the mob swarming over Newgate, he picks out
the two sons again, close-up, providing a momentary human glimpse into the
hearts of the rioters:

> But the anguish and suffering of the two sons of one of these men,
> when they heard, or fancied that they heard, their father's voice, is past
> description. After wringing their hands and rushing to and fro as if
> they were stark mad, one mounted on the shoulders of his brother and
> tried to clamber up the face of the high wall, guarded at the top with
> spikes and points of iron. And when he fell among the crowd, he was
> not deterred by his bruises, but mounted up again, and fell again, and,
> when he found the feat impossible, began to beat the stones and tear
> them with his hands, as if he could that way make a breach in the strong
> building, and force a passage in. At last, they clove their way among the
> mob about the door, though many men, a dozen times their match, had
> tried in vain to do so, and were seen, in – yes, in – the fire, striving to
> prize it down, with crowbars.   (*BR* 64, 536)

When reproved by John Forster for giving too sympathetic an account of Lord
George Gordon, who had provoked the riots, Dickens insisted that he 'must
have been at heart a kind man, and a lover of the despised and rejected, after
his own fashion' (*L* 2: 294–5). If *Barnaby Rudge* ends with an image of an
inclusive 'bright household world' (*BR* 80, 665), then its stability has been won

out of a struggle between different kinds of sympathies, none of them easy to tell apart as natural.

The only other historical novel written by Dickens, *A Tale of Two Cities*, also seems to contrast natural family feeling with darker forces manifested in historical events, but again untangling them from each other proves no easy matter. Although it is often read as a novel structured around a familiar opposition between French barbarity and English homeliness, implying the superiority of measured British constitutional change as against French revolutionary excess, the novel tells a much more complicated story. Bulwer Lytton recognized as much, and, like John Forster in the case of *Barnaby Rudge*, complained that Dickens showed too much sympathy for the revolutionaries (*L* 9: 258–60). Dickens insisted his novel was based on personal testimonies from the time, showing that 'poverty, nakedness, hunger, thirst, sickness, misery, oppression and neglect of all kinds' (*TTC* 3: 4, 279) were ultimately to blame for the upsurge of bloody violence. The personal is political and vice versa. Moreover, the narrator explicitly corrects British assumptions that the Revolution is the expression of some innate savagery in the French people:

> as if it were the one only harvest ever known under the skies that had not been sown – as if nothing had ever been done, or omitted to be done, that had led to it – as if observers of the wretched millions in France, and of the misused and perverted resources that should have made them prosperous, had not seen it inevitably coming, years before, and had not in plain words recorded what they saw.
>
> (*TTC* 2: 24, 246–7)

Nonetheless, the novel does seem to pit a family against the forces of history represented by the guillotine and the Terror. There may be no simplistic opposition between Britain and France, but the Darnay-Manette family are threatened by the revolutionary violence of the crowd, manifested in the unnatural vengeance of Madame Defarge, 'a tigress … absolutely without pity' (*TTC* 3: 14, 375).

Carton's sacrifice makes possible the family scene with which Dickens closes *A Tale of Two Cities*:

> 'I see the lives for which I lay down my life, peaceful, useful, prosperous and happy, in that England which I shall see no more. I see Her with a child upon her bosom, who bears my name. I see her father, aged and bent, but otherwise restored, and faithful to all men in his healing office, and at peace. I see the good old man, so long their friend, in ten years' time enriching them with all he has, and passing tranquilly to his reward.   (*TTC* 3: 15, 389–90)

From early in the novel, however, the family has not been simply in opposition to historical events but bound up with their development. The fall of the Bastille is not just the unleashing of a world-historical force, as it is in Carlyle's *The French Revolution* (1837), a major source for *A Tale of Two Cities*, but also part of its family romance, focalized in the Bastille scenes through the struggle of Ernest Defarge to discover the secret of Dr Manette's cell. As if making the point that this mob is constituted out of individuals with their own hopes and motives, the narrative camera zooms in on the puzzled responses of the seven prisoners released from the gaol and the blank faces of the seven dead victims of the crowd's retribution: 'But, in the ocean of faces where every fierce and furious expression was in vivid life, there were two groups of faces – each seven in number – so fixedly contrasting with the rest, that never did sea roll which bore more memorable wrecks with it' (*TTC* 2: 21, 229). The technique develops the way Dickens picks out the faces of the two sons in *Barnaby Rudge*, but in *A Tale of Two Cities* the family romance is much more central to the historical drama than it was in the earlier novel.

The French Revolution is narrated in *A Tale of Two Cities* by playing out the interrelationship between the families of Madame Defarge, the Evrémondes, and the Manettes. Madame Defarge is not simply an unfeeling savage; her commitment to the Revolution is revealed to be the result of the dreadful suffering of her family caused by the aristocratic Evrémonde brothers and witnessed by Dr Manette:

> 'I was brought up among the fishermen of the sea-shore, and that peasant-family so injured by the two Evrémonde brothers, as that Bastille paper describes, is my family. Defarge, that sister of the mortally wounded boy upon the ground was my sister, that husband was my sister's husband, that unborn child was their child, that brother was my brother, that father was my father, those dead are my dead, and that summons to answer for those things descends to me!'
>
> (*TTC* 3: 12, 354)

Her bitter fury has deformed feelings that Dickens often construes as natural. Her 'brooding sense of wrong, and an inveterate hatred of a class' mean that 'if she had ever had the virtue in her, it had quite gone out of her' (*TTC* 3: 14, 375). She may represent a destructive fury grown out of the distortion of natural feelings, but even at the end of the novel the Revolution itself is still allowed to be associated with hopeful possibilities attached to family affections. So in the cart on the way to the guillotine, a nameless girl holds Carton's hand for comfort in the face of what is to come, but rather than just representing her as an innocent sacrifice to furious resentment, Dickens uses her as a reminder of the original goals of the Revolution and what it was against. As death comes closer, she thinks of her only relative, a cousin, an orphan like herself, who she loves 'very dearly', and wonders, 'If the Republic really does good to the poor, and they come to be less hungry, and in all ways to suffer less, she may live a long time; she may even live to be old' (*TTC* 3: 15, 388). The possibility of this hope proving true is kept alive in Carton's final vision of 'the evil of this time and of the previous time of which this is the natural birth, gradually making expiation for itself' (*TTC* 3: 15, 389). His vision of 'a beautiful city and a brilliant people rising from this abyss' (*TTC* 3: 15, 389) is a prophecy of the future of France that is often neglected in favour of his more personal account of the fate of his own name as it is passed on through the generations of the Darnay-Manette family.

If history, violence, and family feeling are bound up in more complex relations in Dickens than may at first seem to be the case, then so too can domestic spaces often appear threatening, uncanny, and very far from providing a safe haven. Even the most humble sites of domesticity can transmute into homes of horror and fear in Dickens. The sensation novels of the late 1850s and 1860s, some of whose features Dickens built into *Great Expectations, Our Mutual Friend*, and the unfinished *Mystery of Edwin Drood*, had shown how what Henry James called 'the mysteries which are at our own doors' could be more terrifying than any external threat, but the idea had been a long-standing one for Dickens.[3] Frequently it is within the home or from parents and guardians that harm comes in the novels. So, for instance, for all the alien forces that threaten Little Nell on the road of her wanderings in *The Old Curiosity Shop*, not least from the skulking pursuit of Quilp, the moment she seems most at risk is when her grandfather enters her room to steal the money she has sewn into her dress:

> A figure was there. Yes, she had drawn up the blind to admit the light when it should dawn, and there, between the foot of the bed and the dark casement, it crouched and slunk along, groping its way with noiseless hands, and stealing round the bed. She had no voice to cry for help, no power to move, but lay still, watching it.
>
> On it came – on, silently and stealthily, to the bed's head. The breath so near her pillow, that she shrunk back into it, lest those wandering hands should light upon her face. Back again it stole to the window – then turned its head towards her.   (*OCS* 30, 234)

The possibility that it is Quilp or some other sexual predator in the room is barely dissipated when it is revealed that he is only after her money, but the queasiness returns with greater intensity when the reader discovers at the end of the chapter, at the same time as Nell, that the intruder is her grandfather. A perversion of the natural order of affection, the terror of the moment is intensified by Dickens's narration from the girl's perspective, not knowing who it is or what their intentions are.

Dombey and Son may be the novel that marks the beginning of a more detailed exploration of the dark mysteries that haunt family relations. Soon after its inquiry into 'what Nature is', the narrative voice seems to anticipate the Jamesian definition of the sensation novel:

> Oh for a good spirit who would take the house-tops off, with a more potent and benignant hand than the lame demon in the tale, and show a Christian people what dark shapes issue from amidst their homes, to swell the retinue of the Destroying Angel as he moves forth among them! (*DS* 47, 702)

In Florence Dombey's family, there is a 'perversion of nature in their own contracted sympathies' (*DS* 49, 702). The perversion reaches a climax when at the end of the same chapter her father's jealous antipathy to her turns to violence, and he strikes her. She flees the house and into the streets, 'a homeless wandering fugitive' (*DS* 49, 753), as Walter Gay recognizes, although she quickly finds herself safe with Captain Cuttle in the naval instrument store. Like the Marshalsea prison for Amy Dorrit, a much more extensive wanderer than Florence, or even the forge for Pip, the shop is one of several seemingly non-domestic spaces which seem more comfortable than any more conventional idea of home.

Further destabilizing the idea of the domestic nature of women, Dickens created a series of female characters defined by their anger and resentment. These women may seem warped by their exclusion from the magic circle of Dickensian domesticity, but they are not simply omitted from the sympathies of the novels in which they appear. In *Dombey and Son* they are most obviously represented by Edith Dombey and Alice Marwood, who turn out to be cousins, despite being from different ends of the social scale, related not least by their anger and resentment at their position as women. Both have been betrayed by their mothers. Alice's 'thought to make a sort of property of me' (*DS* 53, 813). Her next words offer an ironic commentary – knowingly or otherwise – on Edith's situation:

> No great lady ever thought that of a daughter yet, I'm sure, or acted as if she did – it's never done, we all know – and that shows that the only instances of mothers bringing up their daughters wrong, and evil coming of it, are among such miserable folks as us. (*DS* 53, 813)

Edith is 'the defiant woman' (*DS* 35, 545) whose fury at being bought and sold like a slave on the marriage market is behind her decision to bring down both Dombey and her would-be seducer Carker. In certain respects, then, the unconventional position of such women brings them a kind of freedom of expression, allowing Alice to scoff at Paul Dombey's confidence in the power of his money: 'Do you know nothing', she asks him, scornfully, 'of a woman's anger?' (*DS* 52, 784). Alice, like Edith, has been a victim of Carker's arrogance, 'a short-lived toy … flung aside more cruelly and carelessly than even such things are' (*DS* 53, 813). Both she and Edith are shown to have good reason for their anger, but, unlike Madame Defarge, whose power for sympathy is lost in her resentment, both women remain in touch with what Dickens thought of as their female natures. Consequently, it would seem, neither is easily dispatched from the novel. Alice does die, but the late scenes between her and Carker's sister Harriet are among the tenderest in the novel. The sympathy Edith shows for Florence throughout the chapters overturns the cliché of the wicked step-mother. Although the novel ends with the vision of Paul Dombey playing with his grandchildren by the sea, particularly cherishing his relationship with his granddaughter, the scene between Florence and Edith in the penultimate chapter provides the real emotional climax of the story. In the last of several important scenes of frankness and feeling between women, Edith reveals to Florence that she did not commit adultery with Carker but lured him to the trap that destroyed him. Florence eagerly asks to plead her case to her father, but Edith is more interested in the relationship with her stepdaughter, to whom she 'seemed to pour out all her woman's soul of love and tenderness at once' (*DS* 61, 940). If the scene still seems to define a female 'nature' in terms of the power of the affections, then here, at least, it seems a powerfully redemptive force with no need of masculine affirmation. Edith disappears from Florence's life at this point, but she remains a compelling presence in the ending of the novel, one not conscripted into the domestic circles of the conventional comic denouement.

There is another angry woman in *Dombey and Son*, who offers a kind of comic counterpoint to the fates of Edith and Alice, not least because she is finally recuperated into the happy circle at the end. Susan Nipper, as her name suggests, is a 'spitfire', full of resentment she cannot restrain herself from voi-cing. It is she who bitterly remarks to Polly: 'girls are thrown away in this house, Mrs Richards, *I* assure you!' (*DS* 3, 38). She is also the only person courageous enough to vent her feelings about his mistreatment of Florence to Mr Dombey. Resigning her post, she becomes a free agent, who finally agrees to marry Toots, a man who acknowledges her to be his superior, and not just in terms of feeling: 'If ever the Rights of Women, and all that kind of thing, are properly attended to, it will be through her powerful intellect' (*DS* 60, 917–18). Consequently, he looks to father a long line of daughters: 'the oftener we can repeat that most extraordinary woman, my opinion is, the better!' (*DS* 60, 944). Perhaps, rather like Jenny Wren in *Our Mutual Friend*, who is also something of a spitfire, the idea of a woman intellectually superior to her husband can only be allowed in the comic subplot by Dickens, refusing any serious aspect to 'the Rights of Women, and all that kind of thing'. Susan's anger is quirkily comic enough to allow her back into a family fold, but no such accommodation is provided for the two most striking instances of angry women from later novels: *David Copperfield's* Rosa Dartle and Miss Wade in *Little Dorrit*. Like Edith in *Dombey and Son*, they too both offer resentful critiques of Victorian sexual politics, remaining outside the domestic worlds that are in place at the close of the two novels. David's narrative perspective is continually drawn to Rosa's troubling presence, which he always perceives as questioning him with its 'piercing look' (*DC* 29, 400). What he remains unable to discern is that her anger stems from her betrayal at Steerforth's hand, the friend to whose faults David remains almost doggedly blind. The throbbing scar that David wants to read as a sign of her unstable character turns out to be the product of an angry blow from Steerforth and a physical manifestation of the cruelty with which he has treated her. What should be a warning to David about Steerforth's intentions towards Emily, he chooses to read in terms of his gendered loyalty to his friend. What Dickens's account of Rosa does not provide is the kind of female relationship that Edith finds with Florence. When Emily runs away with Steerforth it is the girl Rosa vows revenge upon. Their final scene together is not one of reconciliation. Instead, Rosa pours out her vitriol on Emily. At the end of the novel, she remains in a mutually tormenting relationship with Steerforth's mother. Miss Wade in *Little Dorrit* is also a 'self-tormentor', but one who is allowed to write her own chapter. 'The History of a Self-Tormentor' reveals her illegitimacy and her relationship with Henry Gowan, another of the self-regarding and indolent young gentlemen in the novels.

These angry female characters remain troubling presences outside the economy of circulation that ultimately contains most of the women in the novels. The critique of the marriage market offered by Edith reappears in Bella's objection to being sold 'like a dozen of spoons' in *Our Mutual Friend* (1: 4, 45), an objection which understandably leaves many readers uncomfortable with the pious fraud practised on her by John Harmon and the Boffins. Bella's objections to being 'for ever … made the property of strangers' (*OMF* 2: 13, 371) gain added resonance because an anxiety about sacrificing young women to the marriage market reappears elsewhere in the novel, for instance, when Sophronia Lammle's women's nature asserts itself enough to save Georgiana, 'on the brink of being sold into wretchedness for life' (*OMF* 2: 16, 409). As objects that circulate in the domestic economy, the role of women may seem designed primarily to clarify relations 'between men'.[4] These relations are most obviously to do with the transmission of property between generations as women pass from fathers to husbands, but women also form a kind of threshold in relation to ideas of adult masculinity. So, Lizzie Hexham, for instance, once Eugene utters the magic word 'wife', becomes the means by which he is able to grow beyond his enervating relationship with his friend Mortimer Lightwood. The two men remain friends, but their relationship is now represented as part of a more diversified domain of relationships and is subordinated to domestic life. Eugene is released from the self-absorbed adolescence of Steerforth in *David Copperfield* or Gowan in *Little Dorrit*. Marriage to Lizzie also allows him to progress beyond his provocative class-based enmity for Bradley Headstone.

Although these patterns of women facilitating transactions between men are present in the novels, they do not seem finally to describe the roles even of the dutiful daughters who eventually become good wives.[5] Dickens often has such women cast out into the world – making them into literal wanderers – before bringing them back to restore order. They rarely restore the family as it existed prior to their travails but rather re-establish the domestic idea on another footing. An early instance of this plot comes with the role of Florence in *Dombey and Son*, a novel often felt to mark a transition from the early works to the complexities of novels such as *Bleak House* and *Little Dorrit*. The novel's title refers both to the name of a firm and also identifies the relationship between father and son which seems to deny even the conventional role daughters could have in the circulation of property, that is, in its transmission through marriage. The novel opens with the father and son framed together:

> Dombey sat in the corner of the darkened room in the great arm-chair by the bedside, and Son lay tucked up warm in a little basket bedstead, carefully disposed on a low settee immediately in front of the fire and close to it, as if his constitution were analogous to that of a muffin, and it was essential to toast him brown while he was very new.   (*DS* 1, 11)

Only in the fifth paragraph does the picture widen to include the first Mrs Dombey, and reveal that she is dying. Her husband heartlessly informs her that he will name the child after himself as he was named after his father. Immediately Paul Dombey is established as a character for whom the family name is more important than the domestic affections.

As the full title of the novel has already made clear, *Dealings with the Firm of Dombey and Son: Wholesale, Retail, and for Exportation*, the issue is not an aristocratic dynasty but the perpetuation of the good name of a long-estab-lished merchant house:

> He had risen, as his father had before him, in the course of life and death, from Son to Dombey, and for nearly twenty years had been the sole representative of the firm. Of those years he had been married, ten – married, as some said, to a lady with no heart to give him; whose happiness was in the past, and who was content to bind her broken spirit to the dutiful and meek endurance of the present. Such idle talk was little likely to reach the ears of Mr Dombey, whom it nearly con-cerned; and probably no one in the world would have received it with such utter incredulity as he, if it had reached him. Dombey and Son had often dealt in hides, but never in hearts.   (*DS* 1, 12)

Dombey's concern with names is suggestive of how far the middle classes were concerned with presenting themselves as the rightful heirs of constitutional change. Rather than acting as revolutionary upstarts, mercantile men such as Dombey seek to mimic the authority of the aristocracy to give their economic power cultural authority. In *Dombey and Son*, this mimicry of aristocratic dynasticism is established early on as pathological. Certainly Dombey's con-cern with the perpetuation of the firm's name cannot recognize even the pres-ence of the daughter. The narrative voice notes with heavy irony that 'In the capital of the House's name and dignity, such a child was merely a piece of base coin that couldn't be invested – a bad Boy – nothing more' (*DS* 1, 13). Marrying Edith, his second wife, seems to express Dombey's desire to have aristocratic approval (she is related to Lord Feenix) and manifest his own power by putting on show a wife with the cool surface beauty associated with the nobility. Eventually, Dombey becomes a version of the threatening aristo-crat of the Gothic novel or the Oriental despot of Eastern tales (he is described as a 'Bashaw' [*DS* 30, 471]). The house in contemporary London becomes a version of the medieval castle, a haunted house and a prison, where his own children, including young Paul while he lives, seem chained to their father's idea of the merchant dynasty. The boy Paul is continually described as 'Old-fashioned' (*DS* 14, 205), perhaps because his father wants to force him into this retrograde idea of family. The climax of this tyranny is reached when the father finally strikes Florence, placing his concern with his own honour above what Dickens sees as the natural affections. Fleeing from the house brings Florence into the homely world inhabited by the Captain Cuttle, Solomon Gills, and Walter Gay. She is able to restore the family, in a sense, but not by returning to the mansion, which is cleared and sold, even the rats quit-ting it. The idea of home requires the demolition of the Gothic castle and the creation of a domestic circle in a more modest space. In *Great Expectations*, Miss Havisham's failure to move on from her father's house – to recreate a domestic space – marks her for death.

Florence's role in *Dombey and Son* suggests the extent to which Dickens understood women to be the agents of this larger social change, even representing it as a transaction between an aristocratic (step)mother and a middle-class daughter. For more than a century, middle-class claims to cultural authority had been predicated on understanding the role of women as the arbiters of domestic virtue as against the showy immorality of the aristocracy.[6] To represent women as the agents of this change did not necessarily grant them more power in society, especially if their agency was primarily figured in terms of their role as household goddesses. Sometimes women are given the power at least to write in Dickens, as is Miss Wade in *Little Dorrit*. Elsewhere in the novel, there are explicit switches to a female narrative perspective, as when the narrator suddenly tells us 'this history must some time see with Little Dorrit's eyes' (*LD* 1: 14, 181) and the account of Clennam's room in Covent Garden is filtered through her experience of it. In *Bleak House*, at least, the primary agent of this transmission of authority from an aristocratic house to the middle-class home, Esther Summerson, is granted more substantial narrative power.

Esther gives her own first-person account as half of what may be a collaborative narrative. She, like Florence, is also part of a transaction involving the figure of an ambiguous aristocratic mother. Esther re-establishes her inheritance away from the grand house at Chesney Wold (one might include Bleak House itself as well) to start a more domestic circle in Yorkshire with Allan Woodcourt at the second Bleak House. She describes her part of the narrative as her 'portion' (*BH* 3, 27). The word implies a share, and so collaboration with the nameless third-person narrator, but it is also a word associated with inheritance, as in *Little Dorrit*, when Dickens speaks of William Dorrit 'bestowing his life of degradation as a sort of portion on the devoted child upon whom its miseries had fallen so heavily' (*LD* 1: 19, 249). A mother who thought she was dead bestowed Esther's story, including the 'degradation' of her early years, upon her, unintentionally. If the other portion of the narrative has a primary concern with the operations of the Law, and its failures to administer inheritance properly, then Esther's is concerned with less official forms of gendered transmission. Could women, as Jenny Wren declares herself in *Our Mutual Friend*, be 'the person of the house' (*OMF* 2: 1, 222)? Will she remain so after her marriage to Sloppy? The law of *coverture* meant that what property a woman brought to the relationship necessarily passed to her husband on marriage. The turnkey in *Little Dorrit* worries about how to settle property on Amy without her father or any putative husband getting hold of it. He dies intestate, unable to get an answer that leaves him satisfied that what he passes on to Amy will remain hers. Throughout the novel, Arthur is challenged by Mr F's aunt – herself part of the 'portion' left to Flora – suspicious of his designs about her inheritance: 'What he come there for, then?' (*LD* 1: 13, 173). Like many of the women in the novels, when Amy turns her back on her inherited wealth for Arthur the ultimate end of her good work is to deliver what she has to her husband (ironically, perhaps justifying the suspicions of Mr F's aunt).

To return to the point made in the opening paragraph of this chapter, families are far from straightforward in Dickens's fictions. From at least as early as Daniel Defoe's *Robinson Crusoe* (1719), the middle-class ideology of the novel had depended upon the removal of parental authority for the hero to make his way in a world where inheritance and a good name were not necessarily enough. This 'freedom' is often described as frightening and not always recovered into any safely respectable form, something no less true of Dickens than of Defoe so much earlier on in the development of the form.[7] When it comes to beginnings, then, a remarkable number of children are raised by surrogate parents.[8] Nor is it simply a case of wicked stepfathers and mothers. Murdstone may terrify David Copperfield, but in *Dombey and Son* Florence is quick to call Edith 'Mama' and finds her affection lovingly reciprocated. Positive examples of surrogacy abound in that novel to throw into relief the failure of Mr Dombey to act as natural parent towards Florence: Polly Toodle, as Mrs Richards, acts as surrogate mother to Florence and Paul; Solomon Gills and Captain Cuttle are surrogate fathers to Walter, Cuttle later for Florence too; Florence is a surrogate mother for Paul, and Walter is a surrogate brother for Florence; Miss Tox becomes a surrogate aunt to the Toodle family, and Cousin Feenix, finally, announces his intention of becoming a 'father' to Edith. Nor does this list exhaust examples even from this one novel. Rather than casting his heroes and heroines out alone in the world to make an identity for themselves, as Defoe tends to do, Dickens often makes them if not the products then the beneficiaries at different times of surrogate relationships, which they risk destroying at their peril.

In *Great Expectations*, Pip seems the archetypal Dickensian orphan, brought up violently by his sister's 'hand' in a perversion of the idea of home, but he comes to realize that the fires of the forge outside, despite their 'red-hot sparks' (*GE* 1: 5, 33), are the most authentic sources of natural feeling, especially once the forge has passed into the affectionate care of Joe and Biddy. In this case, feeling 'ashamed of home' (*GE* 1: 14, 106) is a terrible error. Pip's journey out into the world ends with fever, which puts his sense of identity into serious danger: 'That I had a fever and was avoided, that I suffered greatly, that I often lost my reason, that the time seemed interminable, that I confounded impossible existences with my own identity; that I was a brick in the house-wall, and yet entreating to be released from the giddy place where the builders had set me' (*GE* 3: 18, 462). Pip has dissolved his sense of self by allowing home to become a question of property, 'a brick in the house-wall'. Fixed into an alienating system of property relations when he abandons the security of the forge, the various delusions finally resolve themselves into the face of Joe at his bedside. At the last, then, he is saved by the surrogate relationship with Joe, and, after long years abroad, finally returns to the forge, although it remains uncertain exactly as to whether he finds a home with Estella.

More often in Dickens the surrogate relationships from which the plots are launched do finally resolve themselves into quasi-familial groups, such as the one that clusters around Oliver and the Maylies at the end of *Oliver Twist*. Despite the importance given in the novel to discovering Oliver's true lineage, the quasi-family contains only one blood relation, Rose, his aunt. Even that relationship he insists on redefining in his own terms: '"Not aunt," cried Oliver, throwing his arms about her neck: "I'll never call her aunt – sister, my own dear sister, that something taught my heart to love so dearly from the first – Rose, dear, darling Rose"' (*OT* 3: 13, 438). Rose and Harry, newly married, live in the parsonage with Mrs Maylie. Mr Brownlow adopts Oliver as his son and lives with him and his old housekeeper in 'a little society' (*OT* 3: 15, 451). Dr Losberne also moves to be near them, often visited by Grimwig. 'The fireside circle and the lively summer group' (*OT* 3: 15, 453) is completed by Giles and Brittles, who divide their time between their old duties with the Maylies and the other two households. Likewise, to go to the other end of Dickens's career, *Our Mutual Friend* concludes with another similarly complex little band saved from the general decay. Its plot resolves into two intersecting circles: that around Eugene and Lizzie, on the one hand, and around John and Bella on the other. Eugene manages to secure his father's blessing, although there is the merest hint of aristocratic impropriety against natural affections (as well as showy surface display) in the father's desire to have a portrait of Lizzie painted, albeit muted against the more general affirmation of domesticity in the reformed Eugene. Bella makes peace of sorts with her mother, but there is no doubt that the surrogate parents who sponsor her marriage are the Boffins. Between these groups, it seems, will shuttle the other newlyweds, Sloppy and Jenny Wren. Little societies such as these might be taken as a covert attempt to imply the inclusivity of bourgeois domestic arrangements against the aristocratic insistence on lineage and dynasty, but the middle classes were as concerned, if not more, about blood relations and legitimacy when it came to their family values, not least because of the issue of the transmission of property.

Dickens seems extraordinarily inclusive in this regard as the phrase 'little society' at the end of *Oliver Twist* might suggest.

The same holds true for nearly all the novels in one way or another. If happy heroines seem to be subsumed into the husbands' identities at the end of the novels, the process of remaking the patriarchal family into a safely middle-class form is never quite left complete. Esther ends her narrative with a supposition that leaves the reader wondering about the future in *Bleak House*. Arthur and Amy reimmerse themselves into the open-ended flow of the city in *Little Dorrit*. At the end of *A Tale of Two Cities*, Sydney imagines himself haunting the Darney-Manette family beyond the grave (pity those poor children!). Pip and Estella's situation remains unresolved even in its happy-ending version with its possibility of no parting. In *Our Mutual Friend* all seems well enough between the couples, whatever reservations the reader has about the pious fraud practised on Bella. The groups that cluster together at the ends of the novels, then, may seem to form themselves around a triangle of mother, father, and child, but there also remains the question of their relationship to society at large. Domestic ideology tended to figure each household as an organic cell in the larger family of the nation. Dickens chose to end his final completed novel not by emphasizing this view of the family but with the question of the relationship of his survivors to society. It's precisely the word 'society' that becomes the stumbling block at the end of *Our Mutual Friend* when Eugene and Mortimer discuss how to accommodate his cross-class marriage. Of course, in the chapter that follows, Twemlow's sudden assertion of an idea of gentility as a structure of feeling based on merit rather than birth or money may seem a classic naturalization of middle-class family values, but it scarcely solves the question of Lizzie and Eugene's future place in society. Perhaps they will be safe in the little society presided over by the Boffins, which will include Jenny and Sloppy, one presumes, as well as the Harmons, just as the unusual relationship between Susan Nipper and Toots will remain part of the circle at the end of *Dombey and Son*. The final chapter is another blow against aristocratic ideas of virtue, but it scarcely explains how the 'wonderful energy and address' of a woman Tippins dismisses as 'a female waterman, turned factory girl' will be fitted into society more largely conceived (*OMF* 4: 17, 794).

Chapter 5

Adapting Dickens: 'He do the police in different voices'

From very early on in his literary career Dickens found his writing picked up and adapted for other purposes, not least because of the tremendous selling power of his name. G. M. W. Reynolds, to become the most widely read novelist in Victorian England in the 1840s and 1850s, set off on his career with the serialized *Pickwick Abroad* (1839), which took Dickens's character across to the Continent. The newspaper publisher Edward Lloyd had his first success in 1837 with his *Penny Pickwick*. Sometimes Dickens gave his permission for these adaptations of his texts, but often he was annoyed. Later he was to adapt his own work for public reading. Apart from straightforward adaptation, his writing has also influenced a great deal of other literature, appearing there either indirectly via allusions to his novels, such as those in T. S. Eliot's *The Waste Land* (1922) and James Joyce's *Ulysses* (1922), or more directly when writers pick up and redevelop his characters and their back stories in so called 'hi-jack novels', as Peter Carey did with his *Jack Maggs* (1999), written from the point of view of Magwitch with an emphasis on the violence and exploitation of the imperial city. Between these two forms of literary adaptation, we might add a third, where Dickens-as-literature appears in the story: this category would include Evelyn Waugh's *A Handful of Dust* (1934) and Lloyd Jones's *Mister Pip* (2008), both of which involve characters reading Dickens in a tropical jungle. *Mister Pip* is not only an affirmation of the post-colonial possibilities available in appropriating a literary classic in new circumstances but also a rejection of the sense of late-imperial decline and cultural decay that dominates the Waugh novel. Possibly *Mister Pip* is more a repudiation of Waugh's melancholia than the prolix potential of Dickens.

In all these categories, there is a tension between the creative opportunity afforded by the prolixity of Dickens's own imagination and the position of the novels now viewed as classics of the English language. The heritage industry reproduces Dickens as an icon of greatness available for worship in the present, often with the implication of a fall from former glories and cultural values built into it. The tension between these two ideas of Dickens – endless

84

opportunity and monument to the past – is perhaps most apparent in adaptations made for television and cinema. 'Charles Dickens' can appear in these contexts as a brand affirmation of quality in an entertainment industry as anxious about its own status as Dickens was for much of his career as a novelist. BBC adaptations, for example, are often weighed down by a perceived need to provide a faithful rendition of a 'national' text, as one might expect of a state broadcasting company. Even so, cinema and television from early on in their development as media have often produced powerful and original creative work inspired by Dickens. Alfonso Cuarón's *Great Expectations* (1998), set in the gulf of Florida and New York, instead of the Kent marshes and London, cleverly turns Dickens's parable of the travails of self-creation in a newly commercial society into a film that reveals the continuity of the same issues within post-industrial modernity. This chapter will concentrate on the television and cinema adaptations of Dickens but in a way that asks what light they cast back on novels which in some respects are often more cinematic than the adaptations. Before going on to talk about those examples, however, I'll explore the relationship between the illustrations and the text in the novels; the early dramatic adaptations, including Dickens's own performances of his texts; and then Eliot and Joyce's more covert literary appropriations of the novels.

Dickens aspired to an ideal of collaboration with his readers, which is not to say he did not also wish to remain in control of the relationship. In certain respects, this collaborative ethos meant he thought of his novels as only realized in the performance of reading. Even before they ever reached the public, however, they were almost all also partially interpreted by the illustrations provided for the numbers issued in parts, and later incorporated into the books. Faced with the adverse comments from friends and reviewers about the serial publication of *The Pickwick Papers* – 'We wish him well; but talking of literature in any other light than that of a hack trade, we do not like this novel-writing by scraps against time' (*Fraser's Magazine*, April 1840, in *Collins a* 90) – Dickens often felt obliged in the preface to the published book to gloss over its origins in an illustrated 'hack' collaboration, aligning himself instead with 'the noblest range of English literature' (*OT* 459). The prefaces to the gathered editions frequently emphasize his literary heritage and the unity of design in his work, affirming his status as an author, but the relationship with his illustrators was intensely collaborative, despite his exacting demands.

The original title of his gathering of newspaper and magazine pieces was to have been *Sketches by Boz and Cuts by Cruikshank*. George Cruikshank, by far the better known of the two at the time, also produced the illustrations for *Oliver Twist* and later claimed to have devised many of its chief characters and incidents. After Cruikshank, from 1836 through 1860,

Dickens worked for most of his career with Hablot Knight Browne or 'Phiz' (short for 'physiognomy' – the pseudo-science which related character to physical appearance). Early in 1838, Browne and Dickens went into Yorkshire together to examine the boarding schools there. The exposure of the practice of dumping unwanted children at such places was central to *Nicholas Nickleby*, but the two men did their research together. Browne didn't just passively illustrate Dickens's ideas. The green paper wrappers for the monthly parts (see Figure 3.1), which became so familiar to readers over Dickens's career, were often searched by readers for clues to the eventual outcome of plot, as Dickens put it to Forster in 1846, 'shadowing out its drift and bearing' (*L* 4: 648). From *Martin Chuzzlewit* onwards, the first novel he planned out in its entirety before publication, Dickens gave Browne an account of the whole story that fed into the style and composition of the cover. The illustrations, which appeared in pairs separated before the text itself in the monthly parts, played a crucial part in shaping the response of readers to the narrative. For *Bleak House* and *Little Dorrit*, exploiting a technique he had first used for a plate in *Dombey and Son*, Browne innovated further and produced the 'dark plates' (see Figure 5.1) that in their subtle interplay of light and dark provided a visual analogue for the tangled gloomy words of the novels.

The illustrations placed the numbered parts firmly within Victorian visual culture. They made the novels into a kind of visual spectacle, a process taken even further in the many theatrical adaptations that appeared on the London stage soon after the publication of most of the early novels. Dickens was famously obsessed by the stage and defended its power to uplift, entertain, and educate in 'The Amusements of the People' (*J* 1: 179–85, 193–201). At a speech in 1858, given at the anniversary for the Royal General Theatrical Fund, he claimed that 'every writer of fiction, though he may not adopt the dramatic form, writes in effect for the stage' (*Speeches* 262). He had failed to turn up for a professional audition at Covent Garden as a young man but did have two comedies performed in 1836. Later, he threw himself into various amateur performances and heavily involved himself with Wilkie Collins in the writing and production of *The Frozen Deep*. Despite all of this activity in the theatre, he never actually adapted one of his own novels for the stage. Others were very quick to dramatize his texts for the popular theatre of the time, often before a complete run of a novel had appeared, much to his irritation. The first dramatization was of one of his early stories, 'A Bloomsbury Christening' at the Adelphi Theatre in 1834, and in the 1830s and 1840s, *The Pickwick Papers, Oliver Twist*, and *Nicholas Nickleby* were all turned into popular entertainments, at least sixty of them before 1840. The vibrant characters and shocking events lent themselves to the spectacular nature of

Figure 5.1 'Tom All Alone's', *Bleak House*, no. 14, April 1853. By
permission of the Bodleian Library (ARCH AA d. 40).

Victorian theatre, in which melodrama was a major genre, but as the novels
grew darker and more complex the rate of conversion dropped away. By the
1860s, Dickens was making it clear he would not tolerate any more of these
performances without his permission.[1] There may be no coincidence that by

this time, Dickens himself had entered the market for adaptations through the public readings he began in 1858.

Although he was always concerned about copyright, and the profit to be made from his ownership of the books, Dickens does not seem to have had a strong aesthetic sense of his novels as finalized texts, whose implicit aspiration was some finished authorized form. Serialization enabled him to take account of responses to the novels as they came out in parts and, potentially, to alter them. He seems to have been always excited by reports that his works had entered people's lives and developed their own further virtual existence there. The public readings seem to have grown out of this sense of the interdependence between himself as the writer and his readers in bringing the novels to life, but they also suggest he had a sense of his stories as scripts, which could be realized in different ways. When he went professional in 1858, after years of giving readings in private, he was not without anxieties as to its consequences for his reputation, aware as he was that he had always been associated with a showiness that some commentators found vulgar. Forster, typically, urged him against the move on precisely this basis:

> It was a substitution of lower for higher aims; a change to commonplace from more elevated pursuits; and it had so much of the character of a public exhibition for money as to raise, in the question of respect for his calling as a writer, a question also of respect for himself as a gentleman.   (*Forster* 641)

Dickens was constantly faced with such Podsnappery from friends. The idea of a 'calling as a writer' implied here is one at odds with the performative tendency he displayed throughout his career: the side of Dickens 'opposed', in Bakhtin's words, 'to all that is finished and polished, to all pomposity, to every ready-made solution in the sphere of thought and world outlook'.[2]

Dickens was too restless to think of his novels in terms of finished and consecrated works of art. Not that he didn't feel the pressure of Forster's opinion: he was too aware of his own hard-won path towards respectability not to register doubts about the venture into public performance. To some extent, as we have seen, he compensated for the situation by insisting he was addressing a circle of friends rather than a paying audience.[3] Whatever anxieties he may have entertained about the 'many headed', he was certainly delighted at the rapturous applause he won on 'Working-people's night': 'a more delicately observant audience it is impossible to imagine. They lost nothing, misinterpreted nothing, followed everything closely, laughed and cried with most delightful earnestness' (*L* 7: 244). No doubt Dickens and those who admired the venture, such as his tour-manager George Dolby and his friend the journalist Charles Kent, exaggerated the social reach of the readings.[4] Beyond the middling sort, his audience was mainly at the respectable end of the working classes, probably largely consisting of skilled artisans, who could afford the 'cheap' shilling tickets. The riskiness of the venture may have been more in the eyes of the more conservative among his friends. What cannot be doubted is the thrill he felt at the immediacy of response from his audiences, whatever their social background, exhausting himself by performances that were 'not quite acting', as one contemporary newspaper report put it, 'and yet … a great deal more than reading'.[5] For all his attempts to recreate his audiences as a circle of intimate readers, accompanying him through the texts, his inflection of the text with the verbal idiosyncrasies, tics, and mannerisms of the characters reminded less sympathetic reviewers of a vulgar showman, and certainly exhausted Dickens himself, whose death may have been hastened by the punishing round of farewell readings he gave in 1870. Dickens sacrificed himself physically and risked his reputation at these public performances, but he was also willing to trim and reshape his own texts to meet their demands. Whereas some performances focused on characters such as Mrs Gamp or on particular episodes, such as the courtroom scene from *The Pickwick Papers*, in the case of *David Copperfield* he worked hard to bring the entire novel into a series of dramatic scenes coming to a climax with the deaths of Ham and Steerforth in the storm.For his projected farewell tour, originally intended to contain 100 performances, Dickens added to the repertoire 'Sikes and Nancy', first performed in public on 5 January 1869, although not before trying it out before an invited trial audience on 14 November 1868 at St James's Hall in London. He completely exhausted himself in acting the scene and shocked his audiences by the violence of his re-enactment (*Collins b* 465). The performance threw into relief those violent energies at work in his writing, otherwise organized, dissipated, or disciplined, or at least checked to some extent in the larger structures of the novels.

From early in his career, Dickens participated in processes of reconfiguring and later performing his own works, and the proliferation of the material has been continued by generations of other writers and performers since. Not the least of these were those many working-class autobiographers who saw themselves and their lives in terms of the characters they had encountered in the pages of Dickens (see p. 4 above). This kind of affirmative continuity with Dickensian populism was not one sought by the generation of modernist writers that succeeded Dickens and his Victorian peers. Literary history usually presents modernism as rejecting the sententiousness and sentimentalism of nineteenth-century fiction, but two of the foundational texts of modernism in English, James Joyce's *Ulysses* and T. S. Eliot's *The Waste Land*, were soaked in knowledge of Dickens. Joyce wrote an essay on Dickens for an examination in Italian in 1912. Based largely on this evidence, Joyce's biographer, Richard Ellman, eager to assert the distance between the modernist and the sentimental Victorian novelist, describes its celebration 'of a writer to whom he felt little akin' as 'reserved'.[6] What did arouse 'genuine enthusiasm', even Ellman acknowledges, was Dickens the Londoner:

> Dickens, in fact, is a Londoner in the best and fullest sense of the word. The church bells which rang over his dismal, squalid childhood, over his struggling youth, over his active and triumphant manhood, seem to have called him back whenever, with scrip and wallet in his hand, he intended to leave the city.[7]

Novels such as *Bleak House, Little Dorrit,* and *Our Mutual Friend* to some extent adopt the form of urban encyclopaedia. Their incorporation of a range of locations and different kinds of language, their deliberate collision of high and low culture, and their exploration of a variety of literary forms, are all aspects of Dickens's novels also essential to the representation of Dublin in *Ulysses.* Predictably enough, Dickens's own work plays an important part in the general recycling of textuality that goes on in Joyce's novel: at least nine of the novels make an appearance of one sort or another in *Ulysses.*[8] These might just be regarded as the parodic objects of Joyce's modernist word games – as in the 'Oxen of the Sun' episode's reworking of *David Copperfield* – or a sideswipe from Ireland against an imperial author capable of his own Podsnappery, at least outside the novels, but Dickens's experiments with narrative voice, especially with free double-voicedness, anticipated and perhaps influenced Joyce's own experiments with narrative. Many of these influences seem to come together in the 'Eumaeus' episode of Joyce's novel in the Dickensian space of a cabman's shelter. There Leopold Bloom imagines travelling to London and taking a tour of 'the great metropolis' before he worries about the effects of the 'circumlocution departments'.[9] From the allusion to the infamous bureaucracy of *Little Dorrit,* the passage seems to switch to Dickens's last completed novel. Bloom describes Murphy, the sailor who has earlier been reciting '*For England, home and beauty*', as 'our mutual friend'.[10] The allusion brings Stephen's earlier casual remark about a knife reminding him 'of Roman history' into the horizon of Wegg's reading of 'The Decline and Fall off –' (*OMF* 1: 5, 65) there.[11] What is happening here may be both a dig at Dickens the Englishman and an extension of the scepticism about empire and the glories of the British constitution already present in *Our Mutual Friend.* What it definitely does do is feed off the parodic aspects of Dickens's own imagination.[12]

Turning to the great monument of modernist poetry in English, T. S. Eliot's *The Waste Land* (1922), the most obvious thing to note in terms of its adaptation of Dickens is the fact that its working title was 'He Do the Police in Different Voices', taken from *Our Mutual Friend* (1: 16, 198). Less often noticed perhaps is the more general debt to the nightmarish vision of the city offered in the same novel. To be more specific, the attention Eliot gives to the river full of flotsam and jetsam, to 'the brown fog of a winter dawn' (l. 61) on London Bridge, and to a world where 'death had undone so many' (l. 63) are all aspects of *The Waste Land* that seem to draw on the language and themes of *Our Mutual Friend*.[13]'Fear death by water' (l. 55), after all, is an injunction Rogue Riderhood persuades himself he need no longer heed, convinced as he is that he cannot be drowned a second time, in a novel full of the kind of 'moral sewage' (*OMF* 1: 3, 30) with which Eliot's poem seems fixated. The crowds which 'flowed over London Bridge' (l. 62) in Eliot's poem recall Fledgeby walking into the City 'against a living stream' (*OMF* 2: 5, 272). In the published version of *The Waste Land*, Eliot did not just re-title his poem, but he also asserted his debts to more arcane books such as Jessie L. Weston's *From Ritual to Romance* (1920) and J. G. Frazer's *The Golden Bough* (1890) rather than Dickens's much more accessible texts. Any affiliation with such a close literary predecessor would have been unhelpful, of course, for a poem committed to the idea of itself as a radical break with the past, especially when the predecessor was one so identified with the popular reader with whom modernism of Eliot's variety was equally eager to break.[14]

Ironically, practitioners of the genuinely new medium of cinema were much less reticent about claiming a debt to Dickens than modernist writers, perhaps unsurprisingly given the intensely visual nature of his imagination. As early as 1897, for instance, the Mutoscope Company put *The Death of Nancy* on screen. The choice not only indicates the shock-and-thrills aspects of early cinema but also picks up on Dickens's own selection of highlights from the novels for his readings, feeding similar vaudevillian tastes.[15] In 1909, the Vitagraph Company returned again to Nancy's murdered body, while similar motivations probably lay behind the Hepworth Company's decision to film *Oliver Twist* in 1912. There followed a series from Hepworth with the same director, Thomas Bentley: *David Copperfield* (1913), *The Old Curiosity Shop*, *The Chimes* (both 1914), and, finally, *Barnaby Rudge* (1915). For the last there was a fastidious recreation of London in 1780, indicative of a tendency towards thinking of Dickens as a window on the city's past that has remained strong in adaptations for film and television. The choice of what is perhaps Dickens's least-read novel as the culmination of this series may seem strange, but the reason is surely the desire for the new medium to exploit the gravity of a great author with the serious claims of history.[16] In fact, pressure in that direction had already come with the adaptation of *A Tale of Two Cities* from Vitagraph in 1911, itself followed by another adaptation of the same film from Fox in 1917.

While the use of Dickens as 'heritage' to dignify an emergent cultural form has remained an aspect of even latter-day adaptations, which often labour under a sense of the gravity of what they are attempting, the appeal of Dickens for film and television makers lies also in the visual quality of his imagination. This point was made by the Soviet film maker Sergei Eisenstein in the essay translated as 'Dickens, Griffith, and the Film Today' (1944), the key text in what has now become a lengthy tradition of speculation on the relationship between Dickens and cinema. Eisenstein was responding to comments made by one of the founding fathers of American film making, D. W. Griffith, who, even though he only made one Dickens film, *The Cricket on the Hearth* (1909), had publicly acknowledged a debt to Dickens in the development of his art. Most of Eisenstein's analysis focuses on those scenes cutting between Brownlow waiting for Oliver's return and his reapprehension by Fagin's gang in *Oliver Twist*, but the essay also implies the influence of Dickens on Eisenstein's own more complex forms of 'montage' in films such as *Battleship Potemkin* (1925). There, juxtaposing different points of view in the same scene, as he famously does in the Odessa steps scene when switching between the stone lions and their survey of the violence going on around them, Eisenstein's technique calls to mind the kind of change of perspective Dickens does in the interplay between Fagin and the landlord in the Three Cripples. Certainly, Eisenstein's brief discussion of the 'dissolve' in *A Tale of Two Cities* suggests he was alert to the way point of view in Dickens could be used to give a sense of the dialectics of history. 'How many such "cinematic" surprises must be hiding in Dickens's pages!' was his judgement when this striking cinematic moment (see p. 46 above) jumped out at him as he flicked through the novel.[17]

Before Eisenstein wrote those words, at least some sense of those opportunities had already been taken in the 1917 Fox version of *A Tale of Two Cities* through its exploration of the interplay between the more personal and the more public aspects of the story.[18] Scenes showing the revolutionary crowd as 'a living ocean' have always attracted film makers. They are an invitation to fill the screen with extras and movement. The 1917 film has the crowds swarm in and out of shot. A powerful impression is created of a whole people up in arms, but the film also takes the opportunity to think about the relations between these scenes of mass action and the individuals involved in them. Building on the novel's focus on Dr Manette 'recalled to life', it cuts from the crowds to an additional scene showing the old man working away in his cell. He hears the crowd and looks up from his work, before the film cuts back to the storming of the Bastille.

Figure 5.2 The prisoners carried from the Bastille. Still from 1917 Fox production of *A Tale of Two Cities*. Source: Fox Corporation small press book, BFI Special Collections. Image kindly provided by Judith Buchanan.

Cutting between the public and the private over the next few minutes provides a powerful sense of the interrelatedness of the fates of individuals and the larger aggregations they help make up. When the seven prisoners are carried out into the streets, Dr Manette is originally lost among the others, but then he is carried forward towards the camera, transformed into a symbol of the Revolution, if still confused about what is happening to him (see Figure 5.2).The weapons around him in the shot suggest the possibility that he might find himself imprisoned again, but now within the Revolution: one might even see them as a subtle visual analogue to the grinding machinery which recurs literally and metaphorically in the novel's lexicon. The blade of the guillotine stands waiting for many of the characters in the novel. Other techniques, such as the double exposure that allowed the same actor, William Farnum, to play both Sydney Carton and Charles Darnay, were novel enough to create a buzz in the cinema audience, an effect that the showman in Dickens would surely have enjoyed, especially as it reinforced the novel's exploration of the fragility of individual identities.

Probably no two film adaptations have had as much attention as David Lean's *Great Expectations* (1946) and *Oliver Twist* (1948). The first has been acclaimed to the extent of being described as the only adaptation 'universally admitted to be great film'.[19] Certainly, the opening scenes, with their arresting translation of Pip's encounter with Magwitch, have become part of film history for their brilliant exploitation of eye-level shooting. Some of the changes made to the novel are intriguing. The fact that Pip closing the door as he leaves dislodges the brand from the fire that sets Miss Havisham's dress alight opens up the intriguing idea that her death is his responsibility and perhaps an act of subconscious revenge, but such psychological realism is bought at the cost of the more surreal aspects of the novel. If Miss Havisham is at the centre of Lean's version of the novel, something of the diversity of the novel is lost as a result. The troubling presence of Dolge Orlick is omitted, for instance, and Wemmick's wooden face and strange fortress home is lost in a presentation of him as an ordinary city clerk. What this adaptation tends to omit are those surreal aspects of the story less easy to recast in a mode of realism. Perhaps nowhere is this clearer than in the ending of the Lean film, which uses neither of those originally written by Dickens. Pip now encounters Estella back in Satis House, jilted by Bentley Drummle and on the verge of locking herself away and restarting the cycle. Pip becomes the hero who can rescue her from this sterile fate. Ripping down the drapery from the windows, he disperses the mists that literally and metaphorically dominated the novel: 'I have come back to let in the sunlight!' Estella becomes a virginal bride saved for a version of domestic ideology: the novel offers the reader nothing so clear-cut.[20]

Lean's *Oliver Twist* more successfully finds a way of translating the verbal code of the novel into an equivalent visual register, despite the excision of the Rose Maylie plot from the story and the resulting incoherence of Monks's retention as the villain. For one thing, he brilliantly creates the city in *Oliver Twist* as a place of bold chiaroscuro contrasts, creating in its basic palette the melodramatic effects Dickens invoked in the novel's famous digression on melodrama (see above, pp. 5–6). The buildings themselves are designed in a way reminiscent of German expressionist cinema, one thinks of the rooftops of *The Cabinet of Dr Caligari* (dir. Robert Wiene, 1920) and *Nosferatu* (dir. F. W. Murnau, 1922), as geometric shapes rather than a faithful recreation of nineteenth-century London. Presenting a world at a slant, they give a constant visual analogue for the idea that from his birth Oliver has been thrust into a morally perverted world. I have already mentioned the way the scene in the Three Cripples creates the intensive cross-cutting between points of view that picks up on the thematic emphasis on eyeing in the novel (see Figure 5.3). Even the casting, with Robert Newton's wonderfully exaggerated eye-rolling manner to the fore, works in this regard. Strangely perhaps, given the use of double exposure in a scene where Sikes is haunted by the faces of

Nancy and Fagin after he has committed the murder, Lean doesn't have Bill's victim's haunting eyes appear to him on the roof. Instead, he cleverly translates a metaphor into a realistic detail. As Sikes slips on the roof, terrified by Nancy's eyes, Dickens writes:

> Staggering as if struck by lightning, he lost his balance and tumbled over the parapet; the noose was at his neck; it ran up with his weight tight as a bow-string, and swift as the arrow it speeds. He fell for five-and-thirty feet. There was a sudden jerk, a terrific convulsion of the limbs, and there he hung, with the open knife clenched in his stiffening hand.   (*OT* 3: 12, 428)

In Lean's film, a musket shot from a policeman brings down Sikes. The similes of the lightning and the arrow are translated into the crack of the gun and flight of the musket shot that kills him.[21] Roman Polanski's more recent version descends into mundane realism by having him slip because he is distracted by Bull's Eye's barking. Perhaps the real failure in the Lean film is in his exaggeration of Fagin's Jewishness, which Polanski attempts to redress by giving the role much more sympathetic depth. Lean's emphasis on a distinctive visual style seems to have deadened any ethical reservations he might have had about those anti-Semitic aspects of the original which came to worry Dickens himself. Given that the scenes in the workhouse seem to reference newsreel footage of concentration camps, which must have been disturbingly present to the minds of most audiences in the 1940s, it's hardly surprising that the insensitivity of the representation of Fagin should have provoked riots in Palestine and the USA. Overall, though, Lean's film follows the Dickensian method of striking a dominant motif in its chiaroscuro effects and provides a powerful visual analogue for the literary patterns and narrative techniques Dickens exploited in the novel.

The contrast of light and dark is one licensed in the novel, but a bolder use of colour as a visual code was adopted by Alfonso Cuarón, who chose green as the keynote for his adaptation of *Great Expectations* in 1998. The repetition of the colour, especially in the paintings, gives a sense of a fertility constantly pushing at the limits of the stiflingly artificial world shown elsewhere in the film. Cuarón also makes the bold move of dispensing with Miss Havisham's fiery death, so central to Lean's version. Few film makers are brave enough to excise those highlights that draw audiences to the cinema – whether they've read the novels or not – as they drew them to the readings given by the author himself. In the film, Pip is transformed into Finn, who comes from the Florida gulf but is catapulted into a one-man show and celebrity in New York with the help of a mysterious donor (the escaped criminal Arthur Lustig, played by

Figure 5.3 Fagin, Bill and Nancy exchange looks in the Three Cripples. Still from David Lean's *Oliver Twist* (1948). Source: BFI Stills. © ITV Studios Global Entertainment.

Robert de Niro, who Finn has helped as a boy). The relationship with Estella (Gwyneth Paltrow) is eroticized, as one might expect in a Hollywood film, but her character is also much more sympathetic and accessible than the novel's version. In an interview with Pamela Katz, Cuarón himself said these aspects were played up due to studio pressures. His interest in the novel's exploration of social issues had to be played down. Even so, the film's primary interest seems to be in the limits to postmodern self-invention in a world seemingly made up of mere surface representations, especially in relation to celebrity culture, an idea very much consonant with the novel's concerns in relation to its own historical moment. Ultimately, the film has a positive ending, with Finn and Estella literally holding hands in the sunset. The final words are Finn's, in voiceover, as the camera lingers over the lovers: 'The rest of it, it didn't matter, it was past, it was as if it had never been, there was just my memory of it.' Of course, the ambiguities of the novel's ending are as difficult a problem for the film maker as they are for the critic, but the suggestion that the past can ever simply be assigned to memory seems much more Hollywood than Dickens. Asking how far we should understand Cuarón as adapting David Lean's film, which he told Katz he knew 'by heart', rather than *Great Expectations* only points out how thoroughly mediated the novels of Dickens have become by now, but then this was a situation Dickens himself wrestled with when faced by illustrators and stage adaptations for novels he had not yet finished.[22]

As I've tried to show throughout this book, much about Dickens was future-oriented. For all its persistent acknowledgement of the weight of the past on the present, even the bleakest novels search for change out of stasis and redemption rather than the puritanical credo of the sins of the fathers being passed on to the children. Nor do his novels easily fit into default assumptions about Victorian realism. Those television adaptations with an emphasis on the idea of Dickens as a window onto the nineteenth century rarely do justice to these aspects of his writing. BBC adaptations sometimes seem too weighed down by their sense of responsibility to Dickens as a cultural icon to fully engage with the imaginative opportunities to be found in the novels. For practical reasons, of course, there are limits to what can be done, although computer-generated graphics and other advances in editing technology are likely to lift some of these restrictions. The 1998 BBC version of *Our Mutual Friend*, adapted by Sandy Welch, had a wonderful cast of British character actors, some of whom, like Anna Friel, have gone on to be international stars. A great deal of time and money obviously went into recreating the seamier side of Limehouse Hole and the waterside scenes. The opening shots of Lizzie and Gaffer Hexham on the river were brilliantly lit to convey a world of darkness with an unearthly light playing on the water, throwing the figures of Gaffer and Rogue Riderhood into silhouette as they debate what belongs to the living and what to do with the dead. The discussion between Venus and Wegg in the shop was wonderfully acted by Timothy Spall and Kenneth Cranham respectively, shot in fairly tight close-up, cutting between the faces of the two characters. Even so, the decision to go with the tight-in filming indicates something of what was missed out from the production: any panoramic view of the shop of the sort that Dickens offers at the beginning of the chapter or the surrealism of the somersaulting Hindu baby. The sheer weirdness of the Dickens world is very hard to translate to a televisual code dominated by an aesthetic of linear narrative realism, not to mention practical restrictions of finances and technology. One episode where the adaptation brilliantly steps beyond these aesthetic terms is in its treatment of the pursuit of Eugene by Bradley. There the streets of London are translated in stark black-and-white night scenes across a streetscape that seems like the geometric trap of an Escher painting.

A more sustained attempt to break out of the straitjacket of linear realism was the 2008 BBC *Bleak House* adapted by Andrew Davies, which after an initial one-hour episode was broadcast in punchy half-hour installments designed to recreate the pace of serialization (and, in the same way, it might be slotted into part of an individual's daily schedule). The midweek broadcasts did succeed in reaching an audience of over six million, although there was criticism of the adaptation for trying to turn the novel into a soap opera, effectively defacing its status as a classic. Within each episode the editing and shooting was extremely dynamic, recreating the sense of a world where things don't cohere in any obvious way. Extreme close-up was often used on Lady Dedlock's stony face (played by an impressively glacial Gillian Anderson) and the sweaty visage of Krook (played by the comedian Johnny Vegas). Jump-cutting and other forms of disorienting editing add to the sense of a distracted universe. Perhaps only the omission of Grandmother Smallweed from the story suggests a perceived need to place a limit on the comic exaggeration in Dickens that can tend towards hysterical excitement.

The question for directors adapting Dickens is how to communicate what Eisenstein recognized as his 'head-spinning tempo of changing impressions' (see p. 51). The answer need not involve the sacrificing of content to style. When Dickens showed the squalor and inequity of nineteenth-century London, he did it in a way that made seeing it far from comfortable for his readers. Filming Dickens ought not to be the equivalent of pointing a camera at a National Trust property. The problem of finding a steady point of view was part and parcel of the inquiry in his writing into what ought to constitute natural relations between human beings in society. How should we look at others? In this regard, the ultra-naturalism of Christine Edzard's six-hour adaptation of *Little Dorrit* (1987) may have missed the point, although the sheer intensity and length of her journalistic realism may ironically recreate a discomfort in the viewer.[23] Divided into two parts, 'Nobody's Fault' and 'Little Dorrit's Story', Edzard's film does recognize the issue of point of view, especially in relation to the perspectives of the 'little' woman in Dickens. What it lacks, perhaps, is the element of visual surprise that so often leaps from the page, like the dissolve Eisenstein discovered close to the end of *A Tale of Two Cities* (see p. 46 above). That 'shot' dissolves a scene into a flashback identifying the cause for the present in the arrogance of the past, encouraging the reader to see the figures now making their way to the guillotine as the same aristocrats who were once travelling the route in their carriages. What an opportunity for a film maker!

Afterword

Dickens's world

> When I first entered on this interpretation of myself (then quite strange
> in the public ear), I was sustained by the hope that I could drop into
> some hearts, some new expression of the meaning of my books, that
> would touch them in a new way. (*L* 11: 353–4)

The hope Dickens expressed to Robert Lytton in 1867 provides a suitable
aspiration for an introduction such as this one. Few people come to the novels
without already knowing something of them or about Dickens, 'Please, sir, can
I have some more' being the most common baseline of knowledge. Hopefully
reading this introduction will induce even greater appetite and possibly even
greediness for more. Dickens himself, I've been arguing, had an imagination
of seemingly endless proliferation, of the sort that didn't even rest easy with
the completion of his own finished works, as witnessed by his refashioning of
them as texts for performance in the public readings. Just as those who lis-
tened to Dickens's performances of his characters often struggled to match his
embodiment of them to what they had imagined in reading for themselves (or
being read to by others), so most first-time readers of the novels have already
had the novels mediated through film or television versions, not to mention
the endless recycling of highlights through other media, from London pub
signs through to all kinds of ad campaigns, a process that had already begun
while Dickens was still alive. Recently, a Dickens World has been opened in
Britain, at Chatham in Kent. One wonders what Dickens would have made of
'The Great Expectations Boat Ride' its visitors can experience. A sad parody
of one of the most exciting passages in his great novel? I doubt if he would
have simply been appalled. He would have wondered about his own financial return, no doubt. He would have wandered around its street scenes to see
what people were doing and what the public was making of it. Certainly, it
would also have set his imagination racing to think about new ways to bring
his novels to life. 'Recalled to life' is a Dickensian phrase, and it is constantly
happening to his novels in the world around us. The recent BBC adaptations
of *Bleak House* and *Little Dorrit* have not simply bent the knee to the canon-
ical authority of the text but stretched the resources and ingenuity of their

medium to accommodate the diversity and energy of the novels. However one comes to it, reading Dickens ought to be a similarly invigorating experience. No easy ride down the Thames perhaps but constantly shooting the rapids of the imagination, sharply changing direction, sometimes lulling the reader into a false sense of security before throwing up surprises, these are books written by one of the great entertainers of the English language. The claim has been made before as a snide criticism, but Dickens would have thought there no greater praise.

Notes

1 Dickens the entertainer

1. For details of the readings, see Collins b. An extended analysis of them is given in Malcolm Andrews, *Charles Dickens and his Performing Selves: Dickens and the Public Readings* (Oxford University Press, 2006). See also Chapter 5 below on Dickens and adaptation.

2. For the most extensive account of the idea of the world of the novels and the societies they depict as a huge prison, see D. A. Miller, *The Novel and the Police* (Berkeley, Calif.: University of California Press, 1988).

3. See Wilkie Collins, 'The Unknown Public', *Household Words* 18 (21 August 1858): 217–22, and the discussion by Helen Small, 'A Pulse of 124: Charles Dickens and a Pathology of the Mid-Victorian Reading Public', in James Raven, Helen Small, and Naomi Tadmor (eds.), *The Practice and Representation of Reading in England* (Cambridge University Press, 1996), pp. 263–90.

4. See Jonathan Rose, *The Intellectual Life of the British Working Classes* (New Haven, Conn.: Yale University Press, 2001), pp. 369, 111–14, and 49 and also his essay 'How Historians Study Reader Response', in John O. Jordan and Robert L. Patten (eds.), *Literature in the Marketplace: Nineteenth-Century British Publishing and Reading Practices* (Cambridge University Press), pp. 195–211. For interestingly different assessments of Dickens against Reynolds, see Ian Haywood, *The Revolution in Popular Literature* (Cambridge: Cambridge University Press, 2004), especially pp. 237–8, and Sally Ledger, *Dickens and the Popular Radical Imagination* (Cambridge University Press, 2007).

5. Quoted in Andrews, *Charles Dickens and his Performing Selves*, p. 43.

6. Juliet John's *Dickens's Villains: Melodrama, Character, Popular Culture* (Oxford: Oxford University Press, 2001) begins its excellent analysis of the novels with the judgement that Dickens's 'most radical contribution to cultural politics is his aesthetic practice' (p. 17).

7. See F. R. Leavis, *The Great Tradition* (London: Chatto & Windus, 1948), p. 19, but see also the appendix on *Hard Times*, and, for the more fully revised view, F. R. Leavis and Q. D. Leavis, *Dickens the Novelist* (London: Chatto & Windus, 1970). For Wilson, see 'Dickens: The Two Scrooges' in *The Wound and the Bow: Seven Studies in Literature* (Cambridge, Mass.: Riverside, 1941), pp. 1–104. There has been

a revival of critical interest in the early works, perhaps beginning with Steven Marcus's *Dickens: From Pickwick to Dombey* (London: Chatto & Windus, 1965), but also expressed more recently in John Bowen's excellent *Other Dickens: Pickwick to Chuzzlewit* (Oxford University Press, 2000).

8. John Carey, *The Violent Effigy* (London: Faber, 1973).
9. See Thomas Boyle, *Black Swine in the Sewers of Hampstead: Beneath the Surface of Victorian Sensationalism* (New York: Viking Penguin, 1989). Although the 1860s is often identified as the decade of the sensation novel, *Great Expectations* included, plenty of contemporaries associated the taste for sensation with the popular literature of the 1820s and 1830s. See, for instance, Thomas Frost's *Forty Years' Recollections: Literary and Political* (London: Sampson Low, Marston, Searle, & Rivington, 1880): Chapter XX, 'The Popular Literature of the Present Day', pp. 317–30.
10. W. M. Thackeray, quoted in John, *Dickens's Villains*, p. 122.
11. The two most famous attacks are Henry Mansel's 'Sensation Novels', *Quarterly Review* 113 (April 1863): 481–514, and Margaret Oliphant's 'Novels' in *Blackwood's Edinburgh Magazine*, 102 (1867): 257–80. For a very useful brief account of the phenomenon of the 1860s, see Lyn Pykett, *The Sensation Novel from* The Woman in White *to* The Moonstone, Writers and Their Work (Plymouth: Northcote House, 1994).
12. Charles Kent, *Dickens as a Reader* (London: Chapman and Hall, 1872), p. 87.
13. Mansel, 'Sensation Novels', p. 482.
14. Mansel, 'Sensation Novels', p. 483.
15. The most obvious manifestation of Dickens's commercial sense is his involvement in the campaign for the recognition of international copyright prompted by American pirating of his works.
16. The idea of the painful pleasures of modern life is taken from Andrea Henderson's *Romanticism and the Painful Pleasures of Modern Life* (Cambridge University Press, 2008). Although Henderson is writing about the Romantic period, she describes a pattern endemic to Dickens's fiction of which Wegg's situation seems particularly emblematic.

2 Dickens and language

1. For the authoritative study of Dickens and the grotesque, see Michael Hollington, *Dickens and the Grotesque* (London: Croom Helm, 1984).
2. For a fuller discussion of syllepsis and zeugma, see Garrett Stewart, *Dickens and the Trials of Imagination* (Cambridge, Mass: Harvard University Press, 1974) and his essay 'Dickens and Language', in John O. Jordan (ed.), *The Cambridge Companion to Charles Dickens* (Cambridge University Press, 2001), pp. 136–51.
3. See Woolf's essay 'Gothic Romance', in *The Essays of Virginia Woolf*, ed. Leonard Woolf, 4 vols. (London: The Hogarth Press, 1966–7), vol. I, p. 133.
4. Sigmund Freud, 'The "Uncanny"', in Albert Dickson (ed.) *Art and Literature* (Harmondsworth: Penguin, 1985), pp. 363–4.

5. Mikhail Bakhtin, 'Discourse in the Novel', in *The Dialogic Imagination*, trans. Caryl Emerson and Michael Holquist (Austin, Tex.: University of Texas Press, 1981), pp. 259–422; p. 301.
6. See Matthew Bevis, *The Art of Eloquence: Byron, Dickens, Tennyson, Joyce* (Oxford University Press, 2007), pp. 114–20.
7. Roger Fowler, 'Polyphony and Problematic in *Hard Times*' in Robert Gittings (ed.), *The Changing World of Charles Dickens* (London: Vision, 1983), pp. 91–108.
8. 'The Late Charles Dickens', *The Illustrated London News*, 18 June 1870.
9. See Wayne C. Booth, *The Rhetoric of Fiction*, 2nd edn (Chicago, Ill.: University of Chicago Press, 1982), p. 207.
10. Garrett Stewart, *Dear Reader: The Conscripted Audience in Nineteenth-Century British Fiction* (Baltimore, Md.: The Johns Hopkins University Press, 1996), pp. 15 and 185.
11. On Dickens, penny reading circles and other forms of 'communal reading practices', see Malcolm Andrews, *Dickens and his Performing Selves*, pp. 51–73.

3   Dickens and the city

1. Quoted in *Dickens: Interviews and Recollections*, ed. Philip Collins, 2 vols. (London: Macmillan, 1981), vol. II, p. 326.
2. The content of these walks is published in a series of short pamphlets put together by Susan Gane, full of arresting local detail, including nineteenth-century photographs and other illustrations. For further details, see www.Dickens-and-London.com.
3. Quoted in Jerry White, *London in the Nineteenth Century: A Human Awful Wonder of God* (London: Vintage Books, 2008), p. 65. White's very readable book is the source of the figures given in this paragraph.
4. See Ian Christie, *Early Cinema and the Birth of the Modern World* (London: BBC, 1994), p. 17.
5. See Grahame Smith, *Dickens and the Dream of Cinema* (Manchester University Press, 2003).
6. Sergei Eisenstein, 'Dickens, Griffith, and the Film Today', in *Film Form: Essays in Film Theory*, trans. Jay Leyda (New York: Harcourt, 1977, rpt), pp. 195–255; p. 213.
7. See David Paroissien, 'Dickens and the Cinema', *Dickens Studies Annual*, 7 (1980): 68–80; p. 78.
8. From Oliphant's unsigned review in *Blackwood's Edinburgh Magazine*, May 1862, reproduced in Norman Page (ed.), *Wilkie Collins: The Critical Heritage* (London: Routledge & Kegan Paul, 1974), p. 115.
9. Linda Hughes and Michael Lund, *The Victorian Serial* (Charlottesville, Va.: University Press of Virginia, 1991), pp. 8–9.

10. See Walter Benjamin, 'The Work of Art in the Age of Mechanical Reproduction', in *Illuminations*, ed. Hannah Arendt, trans. Harry Zohn (London: Pimlico, 1999), pp. 219–53.
11. Quoted in Gerard Curtis, 'Dickens in the Visual Market', in John O. Jordan and Robert L. Patten (eds.), *Literature in the Marketplace: Nineteenth-Century Publishing and Reading Practices* (Cambridge University Press, 1995), pp. 213–49; p. 215.
12. Quoted in Curtis, 'Dickens in the Visual Market', p. 214.
13. *Illustrated London News*, 14 May 1842.
14. See the discussion of the ad in Curtis, 'Dickens in the Visual Market', p. 220.
15. Georg Simmel, quoted in Walter Benjamin, *Charles Baudelaire: A Lyric Poet in the Era of High Capitalism*, trans. Harry Zohn (London: New Left Books, 1973), p. 37.
16. Both quoted in Curtis, 'Dickens in the Visual Market', p. 218.
17. Eisenstein, 'Dickens, Griffith, and the Film Today,' pp. 216–17.
18. A similarly misplaced confidence in the mesmeric power of his eyes is shown by the apprentice Sim Tappertit in *Barnaby Rudge* (1: 4, 45).
19. See Benjamin, *Charles Baudelaire*, p. 39.
20. Edward Bulwer Lytton, *Eugene Aram*, 3 vols. (London: Henry Colburn & Richard Bentley, 1832), vol. II, p. 277. See Benjamin, *Charles Baudelaire*, p. 38.
21. See Benjamin, *Charles Baudelaire*, pp. 49–50, and Michael Hollington's 'Dickens the *Flâneur*', *The Dickensian*, 67 (1981): 71–87.
22. The articles were collected together as *London Labour and the London Poor*, 2 vols. (1851).
23. See Boyle, *Black Swine in the Sewers of Hampstead*.

4   Dickens, gender, and domesticity

1. George Newlin, *Everyone in Dickens: Vol III Characteristics and Commentaries, Tables and Tabulations, A Taxonomy* (Westport, Conn.: Greenwood Press, 1995), p. 285.
2. For an exploration of the way the home is contrasted with the aristocratic castle in the Gothic novel, see Kate Ellis Ferguson, *The Contested Castle: Gothic Novels and the Subversion of Domestic Ideology* (Urbana, Ill.: University of Illinois Press, 1989).
3. See Henry James's review of Mary Elizabeth Braddon's *Aurora Floyd* for *The Nation*, 9 November 1865.
4. See Eve Kosofsky Sedgwick, *Between Men: English Literature and Male Homosocial Desire* (New York: Columbia University Press, 1985).
5. For a very useful discussion of the pattern, see Hilary Schor, *Dickens and the Daughter of the House* (Cambridge University Press, 1999).
6. On the role of women and domestic ideology in negotiating the representations of these historical and political changes, see Nancy Armstrong, *Desire and Domestic Fiction: A Political History of the Novel* (Oxford University Press, 1987).

7. Defending the realism of describing characters 'from the most criminal and degraded of London's population' in his introduction to the 1841 third edition of *Oliver Twist*, Dickens appealed to eighteenth-century precedents which included Defoe, along with Fielding, Goldsmith, Smollett, Richardson, and Mackenzie (*OT* 456, 459).

8. See the discussion in Catherine Waters, *Dickens and the Politics of the Family* (Cambridge University Press, 1997).

5 Adapting Dickens

1. Previously, it was more or less assumed that published works were in the public domain and, therefore, available to be put on stage without seeking permission from the author or his publisher.

2. Mikhail Bakhtin, *Rabelais and His World*, trans. by Hélène Iswolsky (Bloomington, Ind.: Indiana University Press, 1984), p. 3.

3. See John Glavin, *After Dickens: Reading, Adaptation, and Performance* (Cambridge University Press, 1999), especially p. 212.

4. They provided the two most detailed eyewitness accounts of the readings: Charles Kent, *Charles Dickens as a Reader* (London: Chapman & Hall, 1872) and George Dolby, *Charles Dickens as I Knew Him: The Story of the Reading Tours in Great Britain and America, 1866–1879* (London: T. Fisher Unwin, 1885).

5. The comment is from the *Bath Chronicle*, 14 February 1867, quoted in Andrews, *Dickens and his Performing Selves*, p. 51.

6. Richard Ellman, *James Joyce*, rev. edn (Oxford University Press, 1982), pp. 320–1.

7. See James Joyce, 'The Centenary of Charles Dickens', in *Occasional, Critical, and Political Writings*, ed. Kevin Barry (Oxford University Press, 2000), pp. 183–6.

8. See Don Gifford with Robert J. Seidman, *Ulysses Annotated: Notes for James Joyce's Ulysses* (Berkeley, Calif.: University of California Press, 1988).

9. See James Joyce, *Ulysses*, ed. Jeri Johnson (Oxford University Press, 1998), p. 583.

10. Joyce, *Ulysses*, p. 580.

11. Joyce, *Ulysses*, p. 590.

12. Tor Rem, *Dickens, Melodrama, and the Parodic Imagination* (New York: AMS Press, 2002) notes in passing the affinities of Dickens and Joyce (pp. 3 and 138).

13. See *The Waste Land: A Facsimile and Transcript of the Original Drafts*, ed. by Valerie Eliot (London: Faber and Faber, 1971).

14. On 6 February 1918, Eliot wrote to his mother to say how he was 'looking forward to lecturing on Dickens'. The following year, 10 July, he thanked her for the 'set of Dickens which is now on my shelf' which she had sent him. See *The Letters of T. S. Eliot, Volume I: 1898–1922*, ed. by Valerie Eliot (London: Faber and Faber: 1988), pp. 219 and 315. See also p. 387, n. 2.

15. For further details of the many adaptations, see Michael Pointer, *Charles Dickens on the Screen: The Film, Television, and Video Adaptation* (Lanham, Md.: Scarecrow Press, 1996), which puts the figure at over 130, although there have obviously been a number of significant additions since its publication.

16. See Joss Marsh, 'Dickens and Film', in John O. Jordan (ed.), *The Cambridge Companion to Charles Dickens* (Cambridge University Press, 2001), pp. 204–23; p. 207. The account of the history of Dickens adaptations above is indebted to Marsh's excellent and insightful essay as well as Pointer's detailed survey.

17. Eisenstein, 'Dickens, Griffith, and the Film Today', p. 214.

18. See the excellent discussion in Judith Buchanan with Alex Newhouse, 'Sanguine Mirages, Cinematic Dreams: Things Seen and Things Imagined in the 1917 Feature Film *A Tale of Two Cities*', in Colin Jones, Josephine McDonagh, and Jon Mee (eds.), *Charles Dickens,* A Tale of Two Cities *and the French Revolution* (Basingstoke: Palgrave Macmillan, 2009), pp. 147–65. For accounts of other stage and film adaptations of the novel, see Joss Marsh, 'Mimi and the Matinée Idol: Martin-Harvey, Sydney Carton and the Staging of *A Tale of Two Cities*, 1860–1939', in Jones *et al.*, *Charles Dickens,* A Tale of Two Cities *and the French Revolution*, pp. 126–45; and Charles Barr, 'Two Cities, Two Films', in Jones *et al.*, *Charles Dickens,* A Tale of Two Cities *and the French Revolution*, pp. 166–87.

19. Robert Giddings, Keith Selby, and Chris Wensley, *Screening the Novel: The Theory and Practice of Literary Dramatization* (Basingstoke: Macmillan, 1990), p. 16.

20. See the discussion in Regina Barreca, 'David Lean's *Great Expectations*', in John Glavin (ed.), *Dickens on Screen* (Cambridge University Press, 2003), pp. 39–44.

21. I owe this point to Garrett Stewart, 'Dickens, Eisenstein, Film' in Glavin, *Dickens on Screen*, pp. 140–3.

22. Pamela Katz, 'Directing Dickens: Alfonso Cuaron's [sic] 1998 *Great Expectations*', in Glavin, *Dickens on Screen*, pp. 95–103.

23. See the discussion in Smith, *Dickens and the Dream of Cinema*, Chapter 8.

Further reading

Ackroyd, Peter, *Dickens* (London: Minerva, 1991).

Andrews, Malcolm, *Charles Dickens and His Performing Selves: Dickens and the Public Readings* (Oxford University Press, 2006).

Benjamin, Walter, *The Arcades Project*, trans. by Howard Eiland and Kevin McLaughlin (Cambridge, Mass.: The Belknap Press of Harvard University Press, 1999).

    Charles Baudelaire: A Lyric Poet in the Era of High Capitalism, trans. by Harry Zohn(London: Verso, 1997).

    Illuminations, trans. by Harry Zohn (London: Fontana, 1973).

Bevis, Matthew, *The Art of Eloquence: Byron, Dickens, Tennyson, Joyce* (Oxford University Press, 2007).

Bolton, H. Philip, *Dickens Dramatized* (London: Mansell, 1987).

Booth, Wayne, *The Rhetoric of Fiction*, 2nd edn (Chicago, Ill.: Chicago University Press, 1983).

Bowen, John, *Other Dickens: Pickwick to Chuzzlewit* (Oxford University Press, 2000).

Bowen, John and Patten, Robert L., eds., *Palgrave Advances in Charles Dickens Studies* (Basingstoke: Palgrave Macmillan, 2006).

Boyle, Thomas, *Black Swine in the Sewers of Hampstead: Beneath the Surface of Victorian Sensationalism* (London: Penguin, 1990).

Brannan, R. L. (ed.), *Under the Management of Charles Dickens: His Production of 'The Frozen Deep'* (Ithaca, NY: Cornell University Press, 1966).

Brantlinger, Patrick, *Rule of Darkness: British Literature and Imperialism, 1830–1914* (Ithaca, NY and London: Cornell University Press, 1988).

    The Reading Lesson: The Threat of Mass Literacy in Nineteenth-Century British Fiction (Bloomington, Ind.: University of Indiana Press, 1998).

Brooks, Peter, *The Melodramatic Imagination: Balzac, Henry James, and the Mode of Excess* (New Haven, Conn.: Yale University Press, 1976).

Buchanan, Judith with Alex Newhouse, 'Sanguine Mirages, Cinematic Dreams: Things Seen and Things Imagined in the 1917 Feature Film *A Tale of Two Cities*', in Colin Jones, Josephine McDonagh, and Jon Mee (eds.), *Charles Dickens, A Tale of Two Cities and the French Revolution* (Basingstoke: Palgrave Macmillan, 2009), pp. 147–65.

Carey, John, *The Violent Effigy: A Study of Dickens' Imagination*, 2nd edn (London: Faber and Faber, 1991).

Carlyle, Thomas, *The French Revolution* (Chapman & Hall 1837).
    Chartism, 2nd edn (Chapman & Hall, 1842).
Clayton, Jay, 'Londublin: Dickens's London in Joyce's Dublin', *NOVEL*, 28 (3) (1995): 327–42.
Collins, Philip, *Dickens and Crime*, 3rd edn (Basingstoke: Macmillan, 1994).
    (ed.), *Charles Dickens: The Critical Heritage* (London: Routledge, 1971)
    (ed.), *Charles Dickens: The Public Readings* (Oxford University Press, 1975).
    (ed.), *Sikes and Nancy and Other Public Readings* (Oxford University Press, 1983).
Connor, Steven, *Charles Dickens* (Oxford: Basil Blackwell, 1985).
Curtis, Gerard, 'Dickens in the Visual Market', in John O. Jordan and Robert Patten (eds.), *Literature in the Marketplace* (Cambridge University Press, 1995), pp. 213–49.
    Visual Words: Art and the Material Book in Victorian England (Aldershot: Ashgate, 2002).
Dolby, George, *Charles Dickens as I Knew Him: The Story of the Reading Tours in Great Britain and America, 1866–1879* (London: T. Fisher Unwin, 1885).
Edmondson, John (ed.), *Dickens on France* (Oxford: Signal, 2006).
Eisenstein, Sergei, 'Dickens, Griffith, and the Film Today', *Film Form*, ed. and trans. Jay Leyda (New York: Harcourt Brace, 1949; repr. 1977), pp. 195–255.
Eliot, T. S., *The Waste Land: A Facsimile and Transcript of the Original Drafts including the Annotations of Ezra Pound*, ed. Valerie Eliot (London: Faber and Faber: 1971).
    The Waste Land, A Norton Critical Edition, ed. Michael North (New York and London: Norton & Company, 2001).
Fielding, K. J. (ed.) *The Speeches of Charles Dickens* (Oxford: Clarendon Press, 1960).
Fitzgerald, S. J. Adair, *Dickens and the Drama* (London: Chapman & Hall, 1910).
Ford, George H. and Lane, Lauriat Jr (eds.), *The Dickens Critics* (Ithaca, NY: Cornell University Press, 1961).
Gallagher, Catherine, 'The Duplicity of Doubling in *A Tale of Two Cities*', *Dickens Studies Annual*, 12 (1983): 125–45.
    The Industrial Reformation of English Fiction, 1832–1867 (Chicago, Ill.: University of Chicago Press, 1985).
Gane, Sue, *Walks in Dickens' London: Exploring Fleet Street*, see www.Dickens-and-London.com (accessed 2003).
    Walks in Dickens' London: Covent Garden, see www.Dickens-and-London.com (accessed 2003).
Giddings, Robert, '*A Tale of Two Cities* and the Cold War', in Ian McKillop and Neil Sinyard (eds.), *British Cinema of the 1950s: A Celebration* (Manchester University Press, 2003), pp. 168–75.
Glavin, John, *After Dickens: Reading, Adaptation and Performance* (Cambridge University Press, 1999).

(ed.), *Dickens on Screen* (Cambridge University Press, 2003).

Haywood, Ian, *The Revolution in Popular Literature: Print, Politics and the People, 1790–1860* (Cambridge University Press, 2004).

Hollington, Michael, 'Dickens the *Flâneur*', *The Dickensian*, 67 (2) (1981): 71–87. *Dickens and the Grotesque* (Beckenham: Croom Helm, 1984).

Hughes, Linda, and Michael Lund, *The Victorian Serial* (Charlottesville, Va.: University Press of Virginia, 1991).

John, Juliet, *Dickens's Villains: Melodrama, Character, Popular Culture* (Oxford University Press, 2001).

Johnson, Edgar, *Charles Dickens* (Harmondsworth: Penguin, 1977).

Jones, Colin, McDonagh, Josephine and Mee, Jon (eds.), *Charles Dickens, A Tale of Two Cities, and the French Revolution* (Basingstoke: Palgrave Macmillan, 2009).

Jordan, John O. (ed.), *The Cambridge Companion to Charles Dickens* (Cambridge University Press, 2001).

Jordan, John O. and Patten, Robert, *Literature in the Marketplace* (Cambridge University Press, 1995).

Kent, Charles, *Charles Dickens as a Reader* (London: Chapman & Hall, 1872).

Leavis, F. R., *The Great Tradition* (London: Chatto & Windus, 1948).

Leavis, F. R. and Leavis, Q. D., *Dickens the Novelist* (London: Chatto & Windus, 1970).

Ledger, Sally, *Dickens and the Popular Radical Imagination* (Cambridge University Press, 2007).

Lukács, Georg, *The Historical Novel*, trans. Hannah and Stanley Mitchell (Harmondsworth: Penguin, 1969).

Miller, D. A., *The Novel and the Police* (Berkeley, Calif.: University of California Press, 1988).

Miller, J. Hillis, *Victorian Subjects* (Hemel Hempstead: Harvester Wheatsheaf, 1990).

Moore, Grace, *Dickens and Empire: Discourses of Class, Race and Colonialism in the Works of Charles Dickens* (Aldershot: Ashgate, 2004).

Nead, Lynda, *Victorian Babylon: People, Streets, and Images in Nineteenth-Century London* (New Haven, Conn.: Yale University Press, 2000).

Newlin, George, *Everyone in Dickens*, 3 vols. (Westport, Conn.: Greenwood Press, 1995).

Every Thing in Dickens (Westport, Conn.: Greenwood Press, 1996).

Oddie, William, *Dickens and Carlyle: The Question of Influence* (London: Centenary Press, 1972).

Paroissien, David, 'Dickens and the Cinema', *Dickens Studies Annual*, 7 (1980): 68–80.

(ed.), *Selected Letters of Charles Dickens* (Basingstoke: Macmillan, 1985).

Patten, Robert L., *Charles Dickens and his Publishers* (Oxford University Press, 1978).

Pointer, Michael, *Charles Dickens on the Screen: The Film, Television, and Video Adaptation* (Lanham, Md.: Scarecrow Press, 1996).

Pykett, Lyn, *The Sensation Novel from* The Woman in White *to* The Moonstone (Plymouth: Northcote House, 1994).

Charles Dickens (Basingstoke: Palgrave, 2002).

Rose, Jonathan, *The Intellectual life of the British Working Classes* (New Haven, Conn.: Yale University Press, 2002).

Rosenberg, John D., *Carlyle and the Burden of History* (Clarendon Press, 1985).

Sadrin, Anny (ed.), *Dickens, Europe and the New Worlds* (Basingstoke: Macmillan, 1999).

Sanders, Andrew, *Charles Dickens* (Oxford University Press, 2003).

The Victorian Historical Novel, 1840–1880 (Basingstoke: Macmillan, 1978).

Schlicke, Paul, *Dickens and Popular Entertainment* (London: Allen & Unwin, 1985).

(ed.), *Oxford Reader's Companion to Dickens* (Oxford University Press, 1999).

Schor, Hilary, *Dickens and the Daughter of the House* (Cambridge University Press, 1999).

Schwartzbach, F. S., *Dickens and the City* (London: Athlone, 1979).

Sedgwick, Eve Kosofsky, *Between Men: English Literature and Male Homosocial Desire* (New York: Columbia University Press, 1985).

Simmel, Georg, *On Individuality and Social Forms* (Chicago, Ill.: University of Chicago Press, 1971).

Simpson, David, *Romanticism, Nationalism, and the Revolt against Theory* (Chicago, Ill.: University of Chicago Press, 1993).

Slater, Michael, *Dickens and Women* (Palo Alto, Calif.: Stanford University Press, 1983).

Charles Dickens (Oxford University Press, 2007).

Charles Dickens (New Haven, Conn.: Yale University Press, 2009).

Small, Helen, 'A Pulse of 124: Charles Dickens and a Pathology of the Mid-Victorian Reading Public', in James Raven, Helen Small, and Naomi Tadmor (eds.), *The Practice and Representation of Reading in England* (Cambridge University Press, 1996), pp. 263–90.

Smith, Grahame, *Dickens and the Dream of Cinema* (Manchester University Press, 2003).

Stewart, Garrett, *Dear Reader: The Conscripted Audience in Nineteenth-Century British Fiction* (Baltimore, Md.: Johns Hopkins University Press, 1996).

'Dickens and Language', in John O. Jordan (ed.), *The Cambridge Companion to Charles Dickens* (Cambridge University Press, 2001), pp. 136–51.

Dickens and the Trials of Imagination (Cambridge, Mass: Harvard University Press, 1974).

Sutherland, John, *Victorian Fiction: Writers, Publishers, Readers* (Basingstoke: Macmillan, 1995).

Tambling, Jeremy, *Dickens, Violence and the Modern State: Dreams of the Scaffold* (Basingstoke: Macmillan, 1995).

Going Astray: Dickens and London (Harlow: Pearson Longman, 2009).

Tomalin, Claire, *The Invisible Woman: The Story of Nelly Ternan and Charles Dickens* (London: Penguin, 1991).

Trotter, David, *Circulation: Defoe, Dickens, and the Economies of the Novel* (Basingstoke: Macmillan, 1988).

Waters, Catherine, *Dickens and the Politics of the Family* (Cambridge University Press, 1997).

White, Jerry, *London in the Nineteenth Century: A Human Awful Wonder of God* (London: Vintage, 2008).

Wilson, Edmund, 'Dickens: The Two Scrooges', in *The Wound and the Bow: Seven Studies in Literature* (Cambridge, Mass.: Riverside, 1941), pp. 1–104.

Index

Cambridge Introductions to ...

Authors

Topics